W9-BZF-989

Saint Peter's University Library
Withdrawn

ELEMENTARY SCIENCE ACTIVITIES

FOR EVERY MONTH

OF THE SCHOOL YEAR

Dorothea Allen

Parker Publishing Company, Inc.   West Nyack, New York

© 1981 *by*

Parker Publishing Company, Inc.

West Nyack, New York

*All rights reserved. No part of this
book may be reproduced in any form
or by any means, without permission
in writing from the publisher.*

Library of Congress Cataloging in Publication Data

Allen, Dorothea.
    Elementary science activities for every month
of the school year.

    Bibliography: p.
    Includes index.
    1. Science—Study and teaching (Elementary)—
Handbooks, manuals, etc. I. Title.
LB1585.A45   372.3'5044   81-9503
                               AACR2

ISBN 0-13-259952-X

Printed in the United States of America

LB
1585
A15

To Marguerite, Carolyn, and Robert

Also by the Author

Biology Teacher's Desk Book

How This Resource Book Will Save Time and Energy for the Teacher

Elementary school students exhibit an overwhelming enthusiasm for science classes in which they are cast in the role of active learners. They find excitement in hands-on experiences that afford them an opportunity for personal involvement in topics being studied, and they enjoy most those activities which present challenging and problem-solving situations.

In keeping with the unique nature of the elementary school science curriculum, the activities included must cover a wide range of student interests and provide for diverse ability and maturity levels. They must encompass a variety of kinds of activity as well as of topic, be simple in design, and employ only such materials as are easy to obtain and easy to handle. Each activity should be relevant and within the scope of the students' ability to manipulate and understand, and emphasis should be placed on topics rather than on generalizations. Those activities which have been found to evoke the greatest student interest enhance the overall program and are imbued with some significant features:

- They are of appropriate length to forestall student boredom.
- They present challenges without being so difficult as to create frustrations.
- They provide pleasurable and satisfying experiences.
- They are open-ended and encourage further study and/or application.
- They are simple enough for students to engage in without an excessive amount of teacher input.
- They provide opportunities for students to gain familiarity with the metric system by employing its use in all matters relating to measurements of length, weight, and volume.

- They allow for some degree of adaptation and creativity.
- They arouse and encourage student curiosity about some familiar phenomenon or some heretofore unnoticed aspect of the student's world.
- They make use of simple materials so that the main thrust of the activity is not obscured by the employment of sophisticated equipment and complicated mechanisms.

This learning-by-doing approach promotes the development of student abilities for recognition and understanding of basic scientific concepts and principles far more effectively than does a mere reading, talking, or other descriptive exposure. But it also poses a problem—it makes heavy demands on teacher time, energy, and resources to provide an ample supply of varied and suitable activities for employment throughout the school year. *Elementary Science Activities for Every Month of the School Year* is designed to help solve this dilemma.

Activities included in this volume have been selected on the basis of their ability to help students grow in basic science skills and knowledge, to develop further their innate curiosity, to extend their experience in thinking and reasoning, and to provide exposure to scientific concepts that will grow and be reinforced with each involvement, until eventually a soundly based feeling and appreciation of science and of the scientific method evolve. The activities are versatile in use for individuals, small groups, or entire classes. They recognize the potential of several learning centers—the classroom, a field setting or other outdoor site, and the home—with activities initiated in one setting often being carried over to another for continuation or completion. The use of simple materials is stressed and the teaching potential of common substances such as air, water, sand, snowflakes, leaves, balloons, and mothballs is realized in novel as well as in traditional approaches to beginning science activities.

Although this volume is basically a treasure chest of activities associated with seasonal changes, calendar events, and some general consensus of the sequencing of topics studied in an elementary science curriculum, there is great flexibility for employment and scheduling of specific activities. Keeping in mind the students and the groups involved, local conditions and geographical factors of the area, and other pertinent criteria, suitable and timely activities may be selected to tailor a program for each classroom.

The activities have been planned for multipurpose employment. They may be used to introduce or to review related topics studied as part of an established science program, to generate interest and enthusiasm for study topics or situations of relevance, or to supplement, enrich, or extend associated learning experiences. If teacher-initiated, an activity may be further enhanced by its introduction as a personal invitation to "Let's do an experiment," "Let's take a field trip," or "Let's find out what will happen if ...." Each should be viewed as an exciting adventure which asks *"How?"* or *"Why?"* of some phenomenon, be it representative of the living or of the nonliving world that is encompassed by what we term *science*.

Guidelines and easy-to-follow directions for activities are organized within chapters which highlight the development of one key aspect of scientific endeavor per month. Designated areas of concentration include:

> *September* activities for developing an awareness of science and for stimulating an interest in its study
>
> *October* activities for developing and practicing skills of observation
>
> *November* activities for developing skills for sorting and classifying
>
> *December* activities for collecting, analyzing, and interpreting data
>
> *January* activities for initiating students to the thrill and excitement of making discoveries
>
> *February* activities for planning and conducting experiments
>
> *March* activities for performing demonstrations by students

April activities for investigating and employing practical applications of science

May activities for engaging in individual and group projects

June activities for participating in science experiences for fun and enjoyment.

Additional activities for each month are also included to review and reinforce previous learning and to serve a variety of special interests. Some activities, presented to highlight the point of emphasis for a specified month, might also be adapted for use in situations having a different approach. Their interchangeability, as in the case of an "experiment" design being adapted for use as a student demonstration or special study project, adds to their versatility in use. Extensive and wise use of these features will help to achieve the maximum benefits available from this built-in flexibility of the format.

It has been the experience of many elementary teachers that, where a student-centered/activity-oriented science program prevails, students thrive and often cite science as their favorite study. By bringing the study to life via hands-on experiences, *activity* makes the learning dynamic and meaningful, with high motivation to learn, to understand, and to appreciate scientific knowledge and relationships. And the activities presented for each month guide the student progressively toward achieving greater independence and responsibility for his own self-learning from the beginning to the end of the school year.

Elementary Science Activities for Every Month of the School Year offers a comprehensive and practical resource and reference book to all teachers who would teach elementary science in an innovative and meaningful way. A collection of selected activities geared to elementary school students, it will provide you with enough varied and worthwhile activities to use for every occasion during the month and throughout the school year—and with a double bonus: fun-filled and satisfying experiences for your students and simple, easy, and time-saving methods for you!

Dorothea Allen

Table of Contents

Activities Involving Data From Measurements (95). Timing A "Snail's Pace." Charting the Growth Rate of Different Leaf Sections. Mapping Isotherms in a Classroom. Graphing Animal Growth Curves. Relating Shrinkage to Early Mountain Formation. **Activities That are Seasonal (99).** Mapping a Winter Constellation. Finding the Temperature at Which Frogs Hibernate. Observing Birds at a Birdfeeding Station. Making a Silver Christmas Tree. Finding the Length of a Day. **Activities Involving Interpretation of Data (103).** Counting Stars in the Sky. Comparing Heights of Boys and Girls in the Class. Finding Differences in the Length of Seeds. Comparing Head Measurements. Finding the Number of Insects Devoured by a Pitcher Plant. Checking the Caloric Intake in Foods Per Day. **Activities Involving Observations and Measurements That Are Relative (107).** Measuring the Brightness of an Electric Light Bulb. Weighing Objects Submerged in Water. Movement of the Moon During Its Phase Changes. Boiling Water by Cooling It. **Activities That Illustrate Limitations of Sense-Perceived Observations (110).** Interpreting Visual Sensations. Reporting Temperature Changes. Seeing a Curved Pattern Formed by Straight Lines. Finding the Shapes of the Moon. Observing Still Pictures in Rapid Motion Blend into One. Creating an Illusion of Motion with Still Pictures.

Activities Investigating Scientific Principles and Phenomena (118). How Much Change in Size Occurs When a Sample of Popping Corn Is Popped? How Does Heat Travel in Currents? How Does Heat Travel Along a Metal Rod? How Does a Jet of Air Propel an Object? What Is the Effect of Heat on Air? **Activities Investigating Living Things (122).** How Can Casts of Animal Tracks Be

February—Activities for Planning and Conducting Experiments, (cont.)

ting the Respiration of Yeast Cells. Determining the Vitamin C Content in Orange Juice. **Experiments That Involve Keeping a Control for Comparison (153).** Investigating the Influence of Heat on the Rate of Evaporation. Determining the Effect of Salt on the Rate of Evaporation. Determining the Effect of Plant Growth Substances on Germinating Seeds. Investigating Corn That "Pops." **Experiments that Are Open-Ended (157).** Investigating the Warming of the Earth by Radiant Energy. Investigating Pressure and Regelation. Investigating Internal and External Body Temperature.

Demonstrations Illustrating Some Important Generalizations in Science (162). Producing Sounds of Varying Pitch. The Effect of Heat on Air Pressure. Creating Air Currents That Can Be Observed. The Force of Inertia. Centrifugal Force. The Effects of Light on a Radiometer. The Relative Densities of Liquids and Solids. **Demonstrations Involving Scientific Phenomena (167).** A Weather "Front." A Ship "Riding the Waves" in a Bottle. Levitation. Static Electricity. An Earthquake. Transpiration of Water from Plant Leaves. **Demonstrations in Which All Students Participate (171).** Location of a Blind Spot. Making a St. Patrick's Day Carnation. How Photographs Are Reproduced in Newspapers. Determination of Eye Dominance. Evaporation as a Cooling Process. Immobilizing Insects. Carbon Dioxide in Exhaled Breath. "Bulging" of the Earth at the Equator. How a Jet Engine Works. Bernoulli's Principle. **Demonstrations Involving Suspense and Excitement (175).** Boiling Water in a Paper Cup. Loss and Restoration of Color in a Dye Solution. Spontaneous Combustion. Archimedes' Principle. Ping Pong Ball in a Funnel. Dancing Mothballs. Fitting Paper Clips into a Glass Already Filled with Water.

1

Activities for Developing an Awareness of Science and for Stimulating an Interest in Its Study

Elementary school students are naturally enthusiastic about learning science. They are fascinated by the "wonders of science"; they examine and probe everything that captures their attention; and they tirelessly ask questions about things they do not understand. In short, they really want to learn and they have strong leanings toward science.

Involving students early in hands-on activities that are designed to link them with the science program provides them with learning experiences that both motivate and give direction to their learning. The nature of the activities suitable for this level, of course, is greatly influenced by two important aspects of the elementary science program:

1. its strong emphasis on the *how* and the *why* of science suggests that the activities selected should feature the method of learning by discovery; and
2. its unified approach to science education prescribes that the activities encompass a broad scope of topics, with great flexibility for presentation and sequencing.

True understanding of all topics studied or of all methods employed may not develop fully until after there have been repeated exposures to the patterns of learning and reiterations of the topics studied in new and different contexts. But it is the development of the student's awareness of what science is and the methods by which it is studied, the encouragement of his curiosity about the world about him, and the stimulation of his interest in learning that are the desirable and much sought-after outcomes of an introductory activities program.

Guidelines for September Activities

To ensure the effectiveness of introductory activities, long-range as well as immediate benefits to the students' science education must be considered. A program, started in September and continued throughout the year, can be developed for elementary science students at various levels, using some very basic guidelines:

- Provide activities that quickly involve all students in the *doing* phase of science.
- Ensure that activities are simple enough for students to engage in without excessive teacher (or parent) interference.
- Select and plan activities that will arouse and/or satisfy student curiosity.
- Provide some transitional experiences that bridge the gap between summer vacation periods and the school year.
- Design activities that make use of simple and inexpensive materials and common substances.
- Include some activities that permit some outside and home participation.
- Enlist the aid of parents to supervise some of the "at home" activities.
- Provide for a variety of experiences via a broad range of activity topics and methods.
- Plan some activities that are keyed to calendar events and other factors appropriate for the area.
- Make provisions for special interests of students.

- Motivate and encourage extensions of study in creative-type projects.
- Ensure student safety while engaging in the activities.
- Provide activities that are suitable for individuals, for groups, and for an entire class.
- Include activities that are concerned with something within the students' experiences to which they can apply the new learning or relate to it in a positive and meaningful way.
- Provide opportunities for students to combine the knowledge they have gained with a feeling of accomplishment.
- Key some activities to the structured program of learning in a manner which imbues them with an authenticity via *real* rather than *contrived* experiences.
- Be genuinely interested in and supportive of student activities, so that students may share with you the excitement of their learning and discovery.
- Concentrate heavily on activities which emphasize development of student awareness of the broad scope of science and of the methods by which it is studied.

HABITAT-RELATED ACTIVITIES

Re-creating natural environments in the classroom is an activity that most students find enjoyable. A variety of natural settings may serve as models, and the resulting environments-in-miniature may take the form of terraria, aquaria, or indoor gardens. If started in September, these can be maintained throughout the school year, during which time students can extend their awareness of the many conditions necessary for supporting plant and animal forms of life and of the interactions that exist between the living and nonliving elements making up a given environment. Different types of environment can be compared and some can be adjusted over a period of time to effect a "balance of nature."

SAINT PETER'S COLLEGE LIBRARY
JERSEY CITY, NEW JERSEY 07306

Initial enthusiasm and sustained interest in an *environment* activity can be motivated by encouraging students to personally:

(1) select the type of environment they wish to re-create,

(2) collect their own specimens and materials to be used, and

(3) arrange and care for the individual and/or group model-in-miniature of a natural setting.

ACTIVITY: PLANTING A TERRARIUM

Even the most inexperienced student can plant and maintain a successful terrarium. For best results he should begin by learning as much as possible about the environment he wishes to re-create. He may consult reference books, pamphlets, and pictures for suggestions and ideas for effective arrangements, but his most valuable and authoritative assistance will come from a visit to the environment to be re-created. First-hand information—the kinds of plants and animals present, type of soil, conditions of light, temperature, moisture, and humidity, and the number and placement of plants in relation to each other—gathered at the site will prove to be invaluable when the student returns to the classroom to arrange his terrarium.

A terrarium can be patterned after a woodland, open field, bog, vacant lot, desert, or other natural setting. Although each terrarium has definite and distinguishable characteristics, faithfully reproduced from the original, there are basic steps that apply to all.

Procedure for Planting and Maintaining a Terrarium

1. Collect soil, small plants and animals, and artifacts from the natural environment.

2. Select a glass container, equipped with a removable cover and of suitable size and shape to accommodate the specimens.

3. Prepare a foundation of suitable base materials, appropriately contoured for the container and specimens,

to provide an interesting terrain with adequate drainage.
4. Moisten the base material.
5. Arrange plants and animals as desired, with care to avoid overcrowding.
6. Maintain the terrarium according to the critical needs of the organisms: light conditions, frequency of waterings, etc.

Remember: drafts, overcrowding, too much heat, too little (or too much) light, and too much water must be avoided. Students must check regularly on all factors until a regimen for the organisms and the conditions of the terrarium has been established.

If animals are included, a thorough knowledge of the animal's natural habitat is needed to reproduce suitable conditions of temperature, moisture, light, shelter, foliage, and provisions for food and water.

The specific requirements for terraria representing different environments will, of course, vary, as indicated by the following popular types.

A Woodland Terrarium

Select a brandy snifter, wide-mouth bottle, aquarium, glass jar, or other container that will accommodate the size and number of plants collected. Place a 2-cm. layer of gravel or other coarse material in the base of the container, and over this drainage layer spread a 3:1 humus: sand planting mixture to a depth of 1 cm. Then fashion an interesting terrain with contour elevations slightly higher in the rear, sloping gently toward the front and/or corners, and with some high and/or low focal point as well. Moisten the planting mixture sufficiently so that it will cling loosely together without caking, and carefully arrange the rooted plants—mosses, ferns, partridge berry, lichens, wild flower seedlings, and small sprigs of mountain laurel and groundpine—in positions similar to those observed in their natural setting. Take care not to create an overcrowded condition, as the plants will grow after they have become established. Add colorful or interestingly-shaped stones, pebbles, or pieces of aged wood for a more attractive appearance, and if an animal such as a frog, toad, salamander, newt, or chameleon is to be an inhabitant also, add a suitably-sized flat rock and a shallow basin of water, recessed and conveniently positioned for its accommodation.

Once assembled in the desired arrangement, the terrarium should be placed in an area that allows for air to circulate and excess water to evaporate when the cover is removed briefly each day. The area should provide sufficient filtered light, with no direct sunlight and a cool temperature, with no drafts. Then, as determined by the needs of the specimens included in the terrarium, it will be necessary to establish a schedule which includes watering, airing, feeding, and trimming out of excess plant growth to ensure the long life and cared-for appearance of the woodland terrarium. A simple design, such as that shown in Figure 1-1, can be constructed and maintained by individual students.

A Bog Terrarium

Collect a sampling of insectivorous plants for the terrarium, and wrap their root systems in sphagnum moss to maintain their fresh condition until the actual time of planting. Then select a glass aquarium or large wide-mouth glass jar suitable for the size and number of plants collected and for their spreading growth pattern. In the bottom of the container place a layer of gravel and cover it with a 2:1 acid soil: sphagnum moss mixture, all thoroughly wetted down to duplicate the conditions of a natural marshland environment. Add pieces of charcoal to absorb odors and reduce any excess acidity, and, if a frog or turtle is to be included, provide a flat rock and shallow pan of water for its accommodation. Now, add the plants: press sphagnum moss around the roots and anchor pitcher plants and Venus' flytraps deeply in the acid soil mixture, but place the shallow root systems of sundew plants closer to the surface.

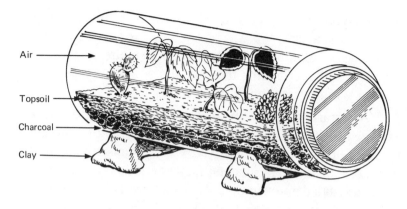

Air

Topsoil

Charcoal

Clay

Figure 1-1. Design for student terrarium in a jar

Allow sufficient growing room for the plants, and spread a layer of sphagnum over all unplanted surfaces to prevent evaporation that would significantly alter the moisture level previously established for this miniature bog environment.

Place the terrarium in a cool location where it will receive some filtered sunlight. Take precautions to maintain a watery environment for the moisture-loving plants and animals: place a removable glass cover over the top of the container to help regulate the moisture level and to provide proper circulation of air for the organisms; mist the plant leaves periodically to prevent their drying; and provide fresh water daily for the animal inhabitants. Also set up a regimen for feeding: using foods which are in the animals' natural diet—mealworms, flies, beetles, and other small insects—feed periodically and promptly remove any uneaten particles to avoid unnecessary fouling of the environment; and occasionally introduce a small insect or a grain or two of hamburger for the insectivorous plants to use as a food supplement. Be alert to the appearance of brown or black areas on plant parts, and remove them as well as overly tall growth which should be pruned away.

There are important watchwords to guide the maintenance of a successful terrarium:

- Avoid overcrowded conditions and incompatible types of organisms.
- Avoid extremes of light and temperature.
- Avoid overfeeding the animals.
- Avoid overwatering the plants.

A terrarium, properly planted and maintained, can be expected to last throughout the school year and to serve as a focal point for student observations of plant-animal interactions, organism-environmental factors relations, and, in many instances, as a demonstration of a natural *water cycle*. A variety of these tiny microcosms will provide for a comparative study and will initiate an awareness of the many microcosms that abound in nature.

A Cactus Garden

Place a 2-cm. layer of washed pebbles in the bottom of a low bowl or other container that will accommodate an additional 7 cm. of planting material gathered from a natural desert environment. If desired, native soil which is rich in organic material can be simulated: in a large container, prepare a mixture that is 50 percent sand, 25 percent decayed leaf mold and humus, and 25 percent rich loam; then spread this mixture in a thick layer over the base layer of pebbles. Position specimens of Prickly Pear, Pincushion, Bunny Ears, Irish Mittens, and other cactus and succulent plants that thrive in desert conditions in an attractive arrangement, anchoring their roots deeply in the sandy planting mixture that has been watered only moderately.

Set the cactus garden where the plants will receive a minimum of 6 hours of direct or fluorescent light, and allow the sandy mixture to dry thoroughly between waterings spaced at about 2-week intervals. To help the plants grow and to prevent their excessive drying, treat their surfaces occasionally with a fine mist of clear water applied with a fine spray atomizer.

A cactus garden requires little care or attention to maintain the conditions that favor growth and flowering of desert-type plants, and this type of environment endures weekend and school vacation periods with no special planning. The cactus garden also provides another biome for students to observe, and, through the activity involved in planting and maintaining this particular environment, students develop an awareness that organic matter and water are basic needs of inhabitants of the desert, as indeed they are of all living things.

ACTIVITY: SETTING UP AN AQUARIUM

Introducing a miniature biome in which the main inhabitants engage in almost constant motion attracts immediate attention and piques student curiosity about the world of plants and animals underwater. While the emphasis is generally placed on the animal forms in these fresh and salt water environments, plants do lend much value to the models and, for interest and authenticity, should be included.

Advance planning and preparation for a successful aquarium-type activity require that consideration be given to the following factors:

- type of aquarium
- kinds of organisms to be included and their compatibility with each other
- size and type of aquarium tank
- location of aquarium tank in the classroom
- recommendations and availability of equipment for providing appropriate aeration, filtration, and temperature regulation
- regimen for proper care and maintenance
- accommodations for weekend and school vacation periods
- familiarity with resource and reference materials

There are many fine references which cover these topics and which students can follow for setting up and maintaining a thriving aquarium. Although care and maintenance activities may become rather routine after the aquarium has become established and stabilized, the fascination of watching and the awareness of events that are in process tend to increase. Fin and operculum activity, feeding habits, schooling, egg laying and hatching, appearance of gravid females, and evidence of territorial ownership exhibited are but a few observations that soon become points of interest for all.

A Fresh-Water Aquarium

Place the aquarium tank in a desirable location that provides natural diffuse light with no more than 1 hour of direct sunlight per day, and a temperature that can be regulated at a fairly constant level of about 20° C. Cover the bottom of the tank to a depth of about 1 cm. with previously washed sand, gravel, or broken seashells. Then place a temporary glass or paper shield over the surface of the base material, fill the tank with clear pond or spring water, and remove the shield. If tap water is used it must be allowed to aerate or to stand for about 48 hours. Finally, add some water plants: *Vallisneria* and *Sagittaria* rooted in the sand, *Elodea, Cabomba,* and *Myriophyllum* weighted at their lower ends with lead strips, and *Lemna* (duckweed), *Salvinia,* and *Pistia* (water lettuce) floating freely on the surface. Install any one of a number of effective filter designs to expedite the initial clearing of the water and the subsequent maintenance of a body of clear water in the aquarium. Additionally, provide a thermometer and heater with thermostatic controls, if room temperature is inappropriate for the animal types selected; an air stone for aeration, if there are insufficient living plants to accommodate the animals to be included; and artificial lighting, if the available natural light is inadequate.

Allow the animals selected for the aquarium to adjust to aquarium conditions before they are actually introduced to the new environment; after opening the plastic bags in which they have been delivered to the classroom, float the bags on top of the water for about 1 hour, or add a small amount of water from the aquarium to the bag until the animals have adjusted and are ready to be added directly to the aquarium. Introduce the animals gradually, a few at a time, taking care to avoid creating an overcrowded situation. One centimeter of fish to 2 liters of water is a good rule of thumb to follow, ... and favorable ratios between plants and animals and between number of organisms and surface area of water should be maintained.

Take care to include only compatible types of fish. To keep the aquarium clean, add some mystery snails, marble snails, or tadpoles of frogs or toads to act as scavengers. If turtles are to be included also, provide a small floating platform for their accommodation.

Although an aquarium needs care and attention, only a small amount of time will be required to establish and perform the following maintenance chores:

- Set up a schedule for feeding the animals.
- Remove dead and/or sickly plants and animals at once.
- Remove uneaten food promptly.
- Scrape and remove accumulated and uncontrolled algae growth.
- Clean filters as needed.
- Circulate and partially replace water in the aquarium approximately once a month.

Partial replacement of water, practiced frequently, helps to keep the aquarium water clean without the need for complete dismantling of the tank, and can be accomplished by siphoning the desired amount of water and gradually adding fresh water to replace the old. The success of the aquarium environment is due primarily to strict adherence to an important three-part guideline:

ALWAYS AVOID OVERFEEDING, OVERPOPU-
LATION, AND EXTREMES OF TEMPERATURE.

A Marine Aquarium

Place a thoroughly washed and rinsed glass or plastic tank of desired capacity in a location which provides a fairly constant temperature of 15-20° C., diffuse light without direct sunlight, and freedom from the fumes of volatile chemicals. Assemble and install an undergravel filter of suitable size and shape for the tank, cover it with a layer of thoroughly washed marine gravel, add natural sea water, and begin operating the filter system. If natural sea water is not available, use demineralized or aged tap water to which *Instant Ocean* salts* have been added to produce synthetic salt water. Then install a power filtration system to further clear the water, and replace any water lost due to evaporation while monitoring the specific gravity of the salt water to maintain its desired salinity.

After several days, when conditions have become stabilized, place selected animals in plastic bags containing water from their natural habitat, and float them on the surface of the aquarium water. Then introduce the adjusted animals— either marine fish or saltwater invertebrates such as small starfish, sea urchins, sea anemones, oysters, crabs, lobsters, or snails—to the marine environment. From this point on, maintain the saltwater environment by monitoring the temperature and specific gravity of the water and by establishing regimens for cleaning, for twice-weekly feeding, and for maintaining the proper water level in the tank.

While specimens collected from a tidal pool and transported in plastic buckets to the classroom will have fewer adjustments to make than those purchased and delivered in plastic bags, most marine aquaria can be maintained for only a short time in the classroom because of the critical need for elaborate cooling and filtration systems. The removal of nitrogenous wastes from the bottom of the tank also creates a problem. While this removal is normally controlled by marine plants in a natural environment, it cannot be duplicated successfully in a school aquarium, and so achieving a balanced salt water aquarium is not a reasonable goal for this activity. The main thrust of establishing and maintaining a marine environment for

---

*available from the Carolina Biological Supply Co., Burlington, N.C. 27215

even a short period is its powerful impact on the arousal of curiosity about a relatively unfamiliar environment and its inhabitants.

New organisms can be added from time to time, and observations made of existing and of changing relationships in the community, of predator-prey relationships, and of various links in a food chain. On a more individualized basis, students can observe the mode of locomotion of a starfish or jellyfish, the budding of a sea anemone, or the feeding habits of some favored invertebrate in response to an offer of a choice morsel of chopped fresh oyster, clam, or other natural food impaled on the points of a forceps.

Plant and animal adaptations to life in the water, as well as their interactions and behavior patterns, can be observed in a marine environment. An aquarium with a variety of plant and animal inhabitants stimulates student interest in a living ecosystem.

NATURE STUDY ACTIVITIES

Students show more enthusiasm for nature studies when they can become involved in doing things with the nature materials instead of merely observing them as specimens. For elementary students whose awareness in the natural world is just becoming awakened, even the simplest of the wide variety of things in nature have great attraction and hold their interest.

September is an opportune month for developing a nature-awareness by making use of simple natural materials, be they representative of plant or animal origin, or be they representative of the natural environment of a park, playground, garden, seashore, rural, or desert setting. Students engaging in activities experience an increased awareness and interest while satisfying a natural curiosity about some common, often well-known object or product.

ACTIVITY: PRESERVING LATE SUMMER AND
EARLY FALL FLOWERS

Carefully select perfect flower specimens of interesting form and colorful appearance, discarding from among those collected any which are wilted, overly-wet, or aesthetically unattractive. Roses, marigolds, zinnias, hydrangeas, or other flowers in season from annual and perennial gardens are suitable and may be used. Prepare the flowers for desiccation by removing the stems, leaving only a 2-cm. stub for ease of handling. Then line the bottom of a cake tin or canister with a 2-cm. deep base layer of drying silica gel and place the flowers individually and in well-spaced positions, with their bases resting on the desiccant material. Gently sprinkle additional silica gel into the container, first around each flower to furnish support, then into the spaces between the petals and within the flower, and finally on top of the flowers, burying them completely in silica gel that extends to the top of the container. Place the cover on the tin and seal the outside edge of the seam between the cover and container with a strip of masking tape. Finally, encase the sealed tin in a coating of parafilm or wrap it in a plastic bag and secure the open end with a twistem-tie.

Allow 8-10 days for the drying treatment to be completed before unwrapping and uncovering the treated flowers. One satisfactory method is to pour off the silica gel onto a shallow tray while gently rotating the tin until the dried flowers are exposed sufficiently to be lifted out of the desiccant. Using a camel's hair brush or air syringe, remove all remaining traces of silica gel, and then, using florists' wire, attach similarly dried stems and leaves to reconstruct the flower specimens for display in a vase or a specimen jar. If specimens are to be stored, include a small amount of silica gel in the air-tight specimen jar and place the entire assembly away from strong light to prevent fading of the specimen. For an extension of the activity, investigate methods of embedding preserved specimens in clear plastic.

While collecting and selecting suitable specimens for use, students develop an awareness of the intricate flower parts and their arrangement, and of the great variety of flower form and color produced by nature.

ACTIVITY: MAKING RAISINS

Select a quantity of fresh, firm, ripe, seedless grapes, sufficient to cover a 23-cm. paper plate. Taking care to avoid bruising the fruit, wash them by immersing in a bowl of clear water, and blot them dry with soft absorbent paper or non-woven toweling. Spread the grapes evenly over the surface of the plate and cover with a four-fold layer of clean cheesecloth that extends 2.5 cm. beyond the outside edge of the plate. Tuck this excess under the plate and staple the cheesecloth to the outside edge, taking care not to exert pressure on the grapes. Place the covered plate in a sunny location that provides direct sunlight and an air flow that permits freely circulating air around the grapes.

After 4-5 days, test one of the grapes; squeeze it lightly between thumb and forefinger. If no moisture remains on the fingers, and if the dehydrated grape springs back when the pressure is released, the proper degree of dryness will have been attained and the grape will be soft and leathery. If additional time is needed, test a specimen each day until the desired degree of dryness has been reached and raisins have been produced.

This activity allows students to produce natural, sun-dried raisins, using a technique that may also be used for other fruits, namely currants, figs, dates, plums, and apricots.

ACTIVITY: MAKING A POMANDER BALL

Organize a group of 6-8 students to make one pomander each from medium-sized fresh fruit, whole cloves, and a mixture of orris root and spices.

Select a firm apple or thin-skinned orange and space whole cloves evenly over its entire surface. Use a thimble to protect the thumb from injury while inserting cloves deeply to make a tight fit. Complete this part of the activity in one session to ensure that the fruit will dry out evenly.

Next make an orris root-spice mixture for six pomanders. Place in a medium-sized bowl and mix thoroughly the following ingredients:

    75 ml. allspice
    110 ml. cinnamon
    35 ml. ginger
    35 ml. ground cloves
    75 ml. orris root

Roll each fruit in the mixture, covering the surface completely. Allow the fruits to remain in the bowl, uncovered, for 3-4 weeks. During this period, sift the orris root-spice mixture over the pomanders from time to time, or turn them gently to ensure maximum and even coverage. The resulting pomanders are dried, shrunken products, made from natural materials, and complete with enticing scents that will last for several months.

ACTIVITY: SKELETONIZING A LEAF

Collect *Magnolia* or other firm, deciduous leaves that show interesting form and no evidence of damage, ragged edges, or insect feeding. Transfer about a dozen perfect specimens to a shallow enamel pan containing a pond water/bacteria/protozoa infusorial mixture, and place the pan in an area which supplies a warm temperature and diffuse sunlight. Allow the soft tissue of the leaves to become decomposed by bacteria in what is a first-level segment of a natural food chain operating in the simulated pond water environment.

After 2-3 weeks, remove one specimen leaf from the macerating chamber and determine its degree of decomposition by holding it under a fast flowing stream of water from a faucet. If the soft tissue does not separate from the supporting tissue, return the leaf to the macerating solution and allow it to remain until sufficient decomposition has taken place. Using other specimens, repeat the testing at intervals of 2-3 days. When all tissue other than the leaf vein system sloughs off when rubbed with a soft brush while being held under a stream of water, rinse the specimens thoroughly and press the skeletons between clean absorbent blotters or toweling. Then immerse the skeletonized leaves in a 3 percent solution of hydrogen peroxide to bleach out the natural color. Dry the specimens once more and laminate by pressing between two sheets of plastic, frame in a suitably sized glass front botanical mount, or make an individual herbarium portfolio using mounting cards inserted into plastic sleeve protectors in a loose-leaf binder.

PHYSICAL SCIENCE-RELATED ACTIVITIES

Some physical science activities may introduce concepts that are totally unfamiliar to elementary school students, but most can be limited to things to which they can relate. Introductory activities that are simple and direct, that are designed to create interest, stimulate activity, and satisfy curiosity, and that focus on topics such as air, water, heat, magnetism, and chemical reactions, serve to expand the students' concept of all that is science by including meaningful aspects of their physical world.

There are also opportunities for developing a familiarity with the proper methods of scientific investigation. Careful handling of materials and pieces of equipment, approaching an activity with a well-defined and well-understood purpose, and practicing appropriate safety procedures can be introduced and established early in the year for continued application to later activities which permit a greater degree of freedom for individuals or participating groups. Hands-on experiences are useful vehicles for developing desirable investigative procedures and for broadening the students' understanding of the great variety of things encompassed by the study of *science*.

ACTIVITY: MAKING A BLUEPRINT

Obtain a smooth-edged glass plate, measuring 12 cm. by 16 cm., 18 cm. by 24 cm., or other desired size, and cut two flat pieces of wood or heavy cardboard of about 1 cm. thickness to match the dimensions of the glass. Select a specimen of suitable size—leaf, fern frond, feather, sprig of evergreen, key, or other interesting shape that can be flattened—and position it on the glass plate resting atop one of the wood pieces. In subdued light, place an appropriate-sized piece of blueprint paper, tinted side down, over the specimen, and cover with the second board. Invert the entire assembly and, holding it securely, transfer it to an area of bright light. Then, carefully remove the top board, exposing the glass, beneath which can be observed the specimen lying on the tinted paper surface. Allow this surface to be exposed to light until the paper fades to a grayish color, then replace the top cover and transfer it once more to subdued light. Carefully remove the specimen and light-exposed paper from between the glass and board layers and place the paper (exposed side down) in a pan of cold water, gently pushing it down into the water to ensure that it becomes thoroughly wetted. Allow it to remain in the water bath for at least 5 minutes; then carefully remove the paper and press it between layers of absorbent paper or non-woven toweling until dry.

Energized by the sunlight, certain oxidation-reduction reactions occur, involving the chemicals with which the paper has been treated. It is the resulting differential color changes that make possible the print of a specimen that has acted as a shield.

ACTIVITY: MAKING OIL AND WATER MIX

Partially fill a clean bottle with 150 ml. of water. Then add 10 ml. of cooking oil, tightly stopper the bottle, and shake the contents vigorously. Set the bottle on a table and allow the contents to settle into a small layer of oil floating on top of a larger volume of water. Repeat the procedure to verify that the very small oil droplets formed by shaking do recombine and form a layer separate from the water molecules. Then, add a small amount of liquid soap or detergent and shake again. Allow this mixture to remain undisturbed for a period of time and observe that no layer of oil re-forms.

When soap is present, oil and water will mix and remain mixed for a long period of time. When fine oil droplets resulting from vigorous shaking are formed in the presence of soap, they become coated with soap and can no longer recombine with similarly coated oil droplets to form a separate layer which floats on the surface of the water. The cleansing properties of a variety of soaps and detergents can be determined for some commonly used household cleaning agents and personal care products.

ACTIVITY: MAKING A COMPASS FROM A MAGNETIZED NEEDLE

With one end of a bar magnet, stroke a large steel sewing or darning needle several times from the middle to the point. Similarly, but using the other end of the magnet, stroke the needle from the middle to the opposite end. Test the magnetized needle in the following manner: drop the needle into the midst of some iron filings spread out on a sheet of white paper, move it around, and pick it up. If iron filings cling to the needle, it has been successfully magnetized.

Next, float a flat cork, with large diameter, in a dish of water. Carefully lay the magnetized needle on the cork and observe the position it eventually takes. The accuracy of the compass can be determined by comparing it with the needle of a pocket compass used in the same location. If agreement is established, assign the letters **N** and **S** to the north-pointing and south-pointing ends of the magnetized needle compass.

AUTUMN SKY-RELATED ACTIVITIES

Current explorations into space highlight the place of the earth in the solar system and in the universe. Their study gives relevance to topics involving the moon, the stars, and the planets. Classroom models illustrating course-related phases of these topics and trips to a nearby planetarium may be further enhanced by selected activities that students can pursue outside the classroom.

The involvement of parents in a follow-up of classroom practice sessions for locating and identifying objects in the evening sky provides the supervision necessary for a successful after-dark activity. Parental aid can be enlisted via special requests sent home together with the appropriate time tables and easy-to-follow star charts. Students are then able to view with their parents some sky shows which continue to be as interesting and fascinating today as they have been since ancient times. Since fall and winter constellations are the brightest, they serve as an introduction and a good beginning point for elementary students to gain a familiarity with the stars and constellations visible during each season.

ACTIVITY: LOCATING THE CIRCUMPOLAR CONSTELLATIONS

Choose a clear, moonless night when the stars are at their brightest, and a location that offers no light interference or obstructions that would hamper clear viewing. Then locate the constellations that are visible in the northern hemisphere, all night long, every night of the year, because they appear to revolve around *Polaris*, the North Star to which the earth's axis points. (See Figure 1-2.)

The Big Dipper

Learning to locate the most conspicuous star groups is a good starting point. To find the Big Dipper, locate the four well-separated stars forming the bowl of the dipper, and three additional stars extending as its handle. The two stars in the end of the bowl opposite the handle are called pointer stars. Follow them to the North Star, *Polaris*, as indicated on a star chart and as viewed in the night sky.

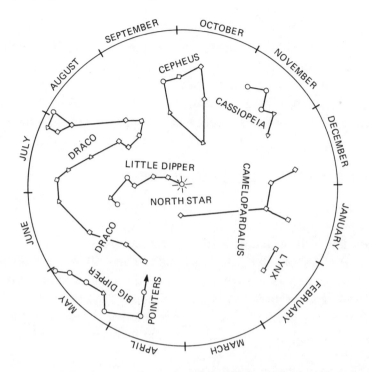

Figure 1-2.   Circumpolar Constellations. Face north and
hold chart with appropriate month at the top.

The Little Dipper

A convenient way to locate the Little Dipper is to begin
your search at the point of *Polaris*, the North Star. It is the end
star in the handle of the Little Dipper. Trace the handle, which
contains two additional bright stars, to the four stars making up
the dipper bowl. To verify the identification of the Little Dipper, consult a star chart.

Cassiopeia

Find *Cassiopeia* by following the pointer of the Big Dipper
to *Polaris* and continuing for an equal distance beyond. The
constellation appears as five bright stars forming what is
roughly the letter W. Check a star chart to verify this identification in the night sky.

The Milky Way

The Milky Way is best seen in September when it stretches brilliantly across the heavens from northeast in *Cassiopeia* in a southwesterly direction into *Cygnus* the Swan. As its name implies, it appears as a luminous pathway extending clear across the sky, and is actually a large galaxy of which the earth is a part.

ACTIVITY: FINDING NORTH BY THE BIG DIPPER

Locate the Big Dipper and spot the two stars at the end of its bowl. Draw an imaginary straight line between these pointer stars and follow it away from the bottom of the bowl for a distance of about five times its length. This will locate *Polaris*, the star which is also at the end of the handle of the Little Dipper, whose direction is approximately true north. It is the star that has guided travelers since ancient times, and which students can use as a guide in determining the direction of north.

ACTIVITY: FINDING SEASONAL STAR
GROUPS AND PLANETS

Use a star chart and face south to view the constellations that appear to rise in the east, cross the southern sky, and set in the west.

September Constellations

Locate the constellations that can be viewed in most northern latitudes during late summer and early fall. Use the designated guide stars to trace the outlines of *Aquila* the Eagle, *Cygnus* the Swan, *Capricornus* the Goat, and *Sagitta* the Arrow. Several bright stars—*Altair*, *Deneb*, and the double star, *Albireo*, can be viewed in these constellations, and can be seen to good advantage with the aid of binoculars.

Morning and Evening Stars

The planets *Mercury*, *Venus*, *Mars*, *Jupiter*, and *Saturn* are bright enought for viewing without a telescope. However, unlike stars, they appear in different locations and cannot be seen in the same position during the same month each year. Frequently one of these planets can be viewed shortly before sunrise, in which case it is designated as the Morning Star, while one that is visible at sunset is called the Evening Star.

The number of these "stars" which are visible on any given date will vary. Consult a calendar or almanac to determine the days when one or more will be visible and search the skies at sunrise and sunset to make the identification.

ATTENTION-GETTING ACTIVITIES

The world of science is filled with intriguing sights, sounds, and unusual occurrences that fascinate the observer. Hence, the interest they create and the curiosity they satisfy make them important motivators for learning. Planning experiences that involve these special attractions serve to capture attention and involve students in their own learning. Initital attention may be developed into a sustained interest in a variety of science topics by introducing varied activities.

ACTIVITY: COLLECTING AND OBSERVING PLANTS AND ANIMALS THAT PRODUCE LIGHT

In a closet or room that is completely darkened, place a pinch of dried *Cypridina* in the palm of one hand and add a few drops of water or a small amount of saliva. With the fingers of the other hand mix these materials together, using a slight pressure and rotating motion to moisten completely the dried material. Then observe the brilliant blue light that emanates from the moistened and crushed remains of what were once very tiny marine crustaceans.

Take a night trip to locate and collect other light-producing organisms. Luminescent mushrooms and other fungi, as well as photobacteria may be found on rotting logs in some moist areas, marine dinoflagellates and other light-emitting invertebrates may be collected at the beach and in shallow salt water, and even some market fish may have some luminescent baceria on their scales and mucous membranes. Dried *Cypridina*, however, are limited in nature to certain areas, primarily the shallow waters off the coast of Japan.

Some light-producing organisms, not generally available during the month of September, will be remembered as familiar specimens ... namely, the fireflies and their larvae, commonly known as glowworms.

ACTIVITY: PRODUCING COLOR CHANGES IN A LIQUID

First dissolve 0.5 g. of phenolphthalein in 100 ml. of 95 percent alcohol. Then pour water into a clean glass jar or bottle to a depth of about 2 cm. and add one drop of clear household ammonia, while swirling the contents gently. Using a clean medicine dropper, add the phenolphthalein indicator solution, one drop at a time, until a pink color appears and remains, despite the continued swirling of the liquid in the bottle. Using another clean medicine dropper, add white vinegar, drop-wise to the liquid, swirling the contents after each addition. Add drops until the pink color disappears. To regain the color, add a drop of ammonia.

ACTIVITY: GROWING A PLANT
FROM AN AVOCADO PIT

Examine the large pit extracted from an avocado and distinguish its upper end, which is always pointed, from its lower end which is always flat. Then select a glass jar of appropriate size and fill it with tepid water. Insert three toothpicks into the seed, equally spaced around the pit and midway between the top and bottom. Then set the toothpicks on the rim of the jar so that the bottom of the seed is submerged in the water. (See Figure 1-3.) Place the jar in an area of subdued light and maintain the water level to ensure that the base of the seed is always submerged.

Exercise patience and maintain both light and water condi-

Figure 1-3.   Setup for germination of an avocado pit

tions as established, until the seed begins to sprout. When roots appear at the lower end of the seed, move the jar to a location of brighter light (such as a sunny windowsill) and continue to maintain the water level as before. Watch as the root system becomes larger and occupies much of the space within the glass jar and as a tiny cluster of leaves emerges from the top of the pit. Note also the appearance of a centrally located stem that grows rather rapidly.

When the stem is 4-5 cm. in length, use a sharp knife to cut off the top half. Discard this portion and continue to replenish water in the glass as needed. Watch next for the development of branches at the point where the stem was cut, and allow it to grow for one more week, while continuing to maintain the sunlight and water levels. Then transplant the seedling: use a flower pot of suitable size and cover the pit completely with a planting mixture of sterilized potting soil, coarse sand, and vermiculite. Maintain the plant in a location that provides good sunlight, and set up a schedule for watering and once-a-week feeding with liquid plant food dissolved in the water. Turn the pot frequently to provide equal exposure of all sides to the sun, and occasionally pinch off newly-developed leaf and stem growth that would cause the plant to appear tall and spindly. If necessary, insert a plant stake to support the fast-growing stem.

If started early in the school year, an avocado pit can produce a good-sized plant by year's end. An established plant, given the same care as any other fine house plant, is easily maintained and can be used for other activities involving plant growth.

ACTIVITY: OBSERVING MEXICAN JUMPING BEANS

Obtain about six seeds commonly known as Mexican Jumping Beans and place them on a table where they can remain undisturbed while being viewed. Note their appearance: small, less than 1 cm. long and only half as thick, and with two sides almost flat while the third side curves inward. Continue to observe and, after a short time, note the rocking motion that begins spontaneously and develops into small irregularly-spaced jumps. Listen for the clicking sounds that come from inside the seeds and that accompany the jumping. Allow the seeds to remain undisturbed for several hours or overnight, and then observe whether the "beans" have traveled from their original positions on the table.

A Mexican Jumping Bean is really the seed of a plant native to Mexico, and the unusual sounds and movements associated with it are due to the convulsive activity of a moth larva that has developed from an egg laid by the parent moth in the flower part of the plant that eventually became a seed. Viewing an empty seed shell will reveal the chamber in which the moth larva, responsible for the jumping activity of the jumping seed, lived while it was undergoing its development.

Learning experiences that stimulate a student's interests, curiosity, and creativity must be offered if lasting impressions are to be made. The attitudes that are developed, the enthusiasm for learning that is engendered, and the on-going synthesis of impressions gathered by all senses in varied topics and by varied methods which complement the structured science curriculum of the elementary school are enhancements which are offered by timely, introductory activities in September.

2

Activities for Developing and Practicing Skills of Observation

Making observations is not a new experience for elementary school students. It is the method by which most of their earliest learning has taken place. Using their senses they have noted a wide array of things, events, happenings, occurrences, and natural phenomena—and consequently they have learned the characteristics by which to recognize things with which they have become familiar and the methods by which to investigate others. As we can see, elementary school students have already experienced some learning via observations that have helped them to gain knowledge and have provided them with a method for increasing it.

But a student's learning in science also is largely dependent upon observations made with his senses of sight, smell, taste, touch, and hearing. Indeed, these first-hand sense impressions are more effective in his learning than are the words printed in his book or spoken authoritatively by his teacher. Science activities that are designed to provide for true observations thus extend a familiar method of learning into the science program. By their multisensory appeal they increase natural curiosity, generate expanded interests, and promote further investigations that may provide some satisfying answers and explanations.

Developing effective skills for making observations is important to a student's success in science. To become a good observer he must learn to concentrate, to be alert to details, and to record and/or describe his observations. In training him to develop these skills, many interesting and worthwhile activities will be needed to provide sufficient practice in the making of sense-perceived observations which focus on the discovery of useful and meaningful information via directed learning experiences.

It is also important that the activities provide students with some latitude for making additional observations. For example, if motivated to ask "How?" or "Why?" or "What if ...?" of an activity or of one of its side issues, they can extend the value of an observation beyond its immediate and specific application to the topic at hand. Consequently, there are long-range values that accompany observational skills; if developed early in the school year, they contribute importantly to the development of a desirable attitude and approach to science and to the art of sciencing.

Criteria for Activities Emphasizing the Development of Observational Skills

Many activities that are directed toward the development of observational skills are timely for October. Close examination of structural details of plant and animal specimens, certain behaviors of organisms available for fall study, natural phenomena associated with current seasonal events, and chemical and physical changes that appeal to the senses all command attention and encourage the making of observations that are both accurate and useful. Good activities for observation are those which emphasize the use of the senses and which suggest additional investigation in answer to questions that may arise from the initial activity. As such, they will probably meet more than one of the following criteria:

- The activity focuses attention on the use of one or more of the senses.

- The activity derives motivational value from its active appeal to the senses.
- The activity focuses on developing an alertness to changes that occur.
- The activity focuses on differences in color, shape, form, size, or reaction of objects or organisms that are otherwise somewhat similar.
- The activity provides sensory experience in which the student participates actively.
- The activity encourages additional questions which involve other aspects of the observation or the topic.
- The activity provides some degree of freedom from the influence of preconceived ideas.
- The activity lends itself to some qualitative or quantitative notation.
- The activity encourages some reporting and/or description of the observations made.
- The activity has no rigid limiting factors.
- The activity provides some flexibility and allows for exploration into an extension of the learning experience.
- The activity provides an opportunity for the student to look long and to ponder; it lets his wonder at what he observes grow.

The aim of activities introduced in October should be to train students to become good observers and, using the skills they have developed, to learn all they can.

ACTIVITIES INVOLVING ANIMALS
AND THEIR ACTIVITIES

Students are genuinely fond of most animals and find them fascinating to observe. Their keenest interest seems to be expressed in those that run, jump, or move about in some way. Watching these animals as they engage in their daily life activities leads the students to the making of many interesting discoveries: that the animals have distinctive characteristics;

that they are active and move about; that they undergo some changes in appearance and habit as they grow, gather food, mature, and produce and care for their young; and that they respond to each other and to a variety of environmental factors.

This natural approach that students have to learning is projected by maintaining some small animals in the classroom. When the program of study provides activities involving purposeful observation of living organisms, early student learning may be extended and reinforced as skills for observation are developed to a higher level.

Many animals, particularly small invertebrate forms, can be reared successfully. Insects are excellent specimens for classroom study because most species are relatively easy to maintain for short-term observation. Organisms that are suitable can be selected on the basis of the following criteria:

1. Animals should be of appropriate size for housing in the classroom.
2. Animals should be adaptable to living in captivity.
3. Animals should be possessed of one or more interesting features to observe.
4. Specimens should be readily available and easy to collect.
5. Specimens should be of nonharmful, nondestructive species.
6. Species should be relatively easy to rear in the classroom, with students assigned a major share of the responsibility for their care and feeding.

Early fall is a good time to bring specimens into the classroom. In most north temperate regions many species of insects, worms, and spiders are still active, and some harmless specimens can be collected in abundance for maintaining indoors.

ACTIVITY: OBSERVING THE ACTIVITIES OF AN ANT LION

Ant lions, sometimes called doodlebugs, are harmless to

man. They are the larval form of an insect of the family *Myr-meleonidae* and are found in abundance in most north temperate regions during October. To locate specimens for study, explore the area for the pits they have made in sandy soil, on the ground near the edges of a building, or under a tree. The larvae live at the base of these self-made pits that appear in the form of inverted cones about 5 cm. in diameter at the surface.

Taking care not to disturb the resident larva, use a broad-base trowel to lift a sand cone carefully from below its apex which is located about 5 cm. below ground level. Then, transfer the cone and some of the surrounding sand and soil to a box which can be transported indoors.

In the classroom, spread the collected material loosely in a flat tray whose sides measure about 5 cm. in height, and observe the activities of the ant lion as it reconstructs its inverted cone. Then introduce a living ant to the sloping side of the cone, as shown in Figure 2-1, and observe the activities of the interested

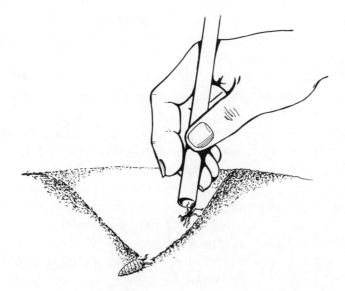

Figure 2-1.   Drinking straw used to introduce ant to an inverted cone housing an interested ant lion

ant lion as it hurls sand upward to undermine the footing of the ant and cause it to tumble into the pit. Continue to observe and focus attention on the functioning of the legs, body, and eventually the jaws of the larva as it reacts to the struggling ant.

To determine the consistency of the doodlebug's response, bait it with a small twig or blade of grass and observe closely. A description or a discussion of the observations made may follow so that students can compare the accuracy and completeness of their observations made individually.

ACTIVITY: OBSERVING THE ACTIVITIES OF HATCHING AND OF NEWLY HATCHED CHICKS

Obtain a clutch of embryonated hens' eggs and a specially designed small chick hatchery, an incubator made from an insulated styrofoam chest, or any other container which provides for some temperature and humidity control and air circulation around the eggs.

Regulate the temperature of the incubator to 38° C. and, to prevent excessive drying of the egg membranes, place a pan of water in the incubation chamber. Then make a small pencil mark, such as an X, on one side of each eggshell and place the eggs, X side up, in the incubator. Turn the eggs twice daily, using the X mark as a guide to ensure that all eggs are properly turned.

On the twenty-first day of incubation, begin to observe carefully the events associated with hatching: rocking of the eggs, cheeping sounds from within, and initial cracking of the eggshell with the egg tooth occur prior to the dramatic emergence of the chick from the broken shell. With care, transfer the newly-hatched chicks to a prepared brooder—a heated box with a constant temperature of 38° C. and side walls high enough to offer protection from drafts and other disturbances. Continue to make observations as the wet feathers become dry, as the chicks' first attempts at standing are strengthened, and as their interest in the surroundings grows.

Place three small dishes—low enough for the chicks to reach easily and deep enough for them to put their beaks into—on the floor of the brooder, opposite the side of the light source. Then fill the dishes—one with fresh sand, one with cool water, and one with food such as grain, mashed hard-boiled egg, or bread crumbs.

Observe the activities of the chicks as they learn to eat and drink, and as they respond to each other. If chicks are kept in the classroom for several days, look for signs of their physical growth and development and of their growing independence and self-confidence. Observe also any signs of individuality in their appearance and behavior, and be alert to changes in their cheeping sounds as they seem to express their feelings of happiness, sleepiness, anger, annoyance, or displeasure.

If possible, place the chicks in a permanent home where observations of their life activities can be continued and described or reported at intervals over a period of time.

ACTIVITY: OBSERVING A HOUSEFLY

Capture an undamaged housefly and mount it on an applicator stick in the following manner: place a drop of glue or melted paraffin wax on one end of an applicator stick and allow it to dry and/or cool. Melt the surface of this drop by touching it with a hot needle and immediately bring it in contact with the back of the fly so that the insect becomes tethered to the stick as shown in Figure 2-2. Using the free end of the stick as a handle, insert it into a block of styrofoam where the mounted fly will be held aloft and ready for use in the activity.

Handling as before, lower the fly over a shallow dish containing fresh water and observe how it protrudes and extends its proboscis into the water. Continue to observe the fly after its thirst has been satisfied, and note how it withdraws the proboscis from the water and retracts it into the mouth cavity.

Hold the applicator stick loosely to permit the fly to move freely over the flat surface of a table, and observe how it uses its

Figure 2-2. Fly attached to stick for easy handling while making observations

three pairs of legs while walking and its antennae while investigating some object or area with which it comes in contact. Use a hand lens for observing greater detail of the fly's structures and their functions which can be viewed more clearly with some magnification. After completing the activity, place the mounted flies in a jar packed in ice, and allow them to remain undisturbed until immobilized. Then snip each stick at its point of attachment to the mounted fly, and return the freed flies, unharmed, to an insect cage where they can be allowed to revive.

ACTIVITY: OBSERVING A WEB-SPINNING SPIDER

Place a large web-spinning spider in a closed container which attempts to simulate its natural habitat. For best results, provide the following favorable conditions: reduced light and a relatively cool temperature maintained in a terrarium or box that contains some leaves, twigs, and, if possible, a fly or two.

Allow the spider to remain undisturbed for 2-3 days in the new environment, and observe its activities during this period of adjustment. Note its inquisitive nature as it explores and becomes increasingly familiar with its surroundings. Use a hand lens to observe the characteristic spider structures and to note how they are used in the performance of some essential life activities.

After a few days, when the spider has become adjusted to the new habitat, darken the room to encourage its web-spinning activities. Observe the activity as it begins (a fine silk thread is attached to a solid support within the enclosure), progresses (the web framework is constructed), and is completed (spokes are added to the framework). Then examine the pattern of the finished web and note the watchfulness of its maker as it awaits any disturbance or tug on the web. If a victim is snared by the network, watch closely as the spider claims its prey.

Prepare a diagram or a string model to show the pattern of the completed web, and, later, trace the web-making process from beginning to end. If the spider is maintained in the box for an additional number of days, observe the conditions that prompt the web-spinning activity, the amount of time required for its construction, the time of day most frequently devoted to the activity, and the frequency with which new webs are constructed and damaged ones repaired.

ACTIVITY: OBSERVING HOW A CRICKET MAKES MUSIC

Convert a small aquarium or a battery jar into a cricket habitat by placing a 2.5-cm. layer of moist sand in the base and a removable screen cover over the top. Then transfer some locally-collected crickets to the prepared habitat, taking care not to create an overcrowded condition. As a general rule-of-thumb, allow about 1 liter of space for two adult crickets.

Maintain the habitat in a cool location where the moist sand will provide an adequate supply of water for several specimens. Feed them on a diet of lettuce, grass, or almost any plant-type of food that is not apt to become moldy, or prepare feeding portions in advance, as follows: prepare a paste by mixing finely-ground oatmeal with a small amount of sugar, skim milk powder, and water; spread the paste on sheets of heavy wrapping paper and allow to dry; cut into 2-cm. squares; and use to feed the crickets every 2-3 days.

Use a hand lens to observe the structural differences in the forewings of the individuals present. Note the presence of a row of teeth, sometimes called a file, on the undersurface of the male's front wings, and a hardened area called a scraper near the end of the file. Observe closely as an adult male "chirps" by rubbing the scraper of one wing across the upper ridged surface of the one opposite. Observe also his pattern of fiddling, and determine the movement of his wings—right over left or left over right—as he produces his musical sounds.

ACTIVITY: OBSERVING MOTH AND BUTTERFLY PUPARIA

Collect moth and butterfly pupa cases, as available during October, from branches of willow or orchard trees, or from branches of other plants in the area. Bring the collected specimens into the classroom for development in an emergence cage, prepared as follows: place a layer of sphagnum moss in the bottom of an aquarium or a box and insert a number of twigs and branches in an upright position into this base layer so that their upper ends do not extend above the top of the container. Glue the pupa cases to upper regions of some of the twigs supported in the sphagnum, and then place a wire screen cover over the box.

Use an atomizer to spray the surface of the pupa cases with a fine mist of water to prevent their drying, and maintain a moderate room temperature until the adults emerge. While waiting for this event to occur, observe the pupa cases for structural details. Use a hand lens to examine their shape, color, texture, and markings. Consult an insect identification guide book to determine if they are moth cocoons or butterfly chrysalids, what is the name of the species that produced them, the approximate time required for their pupation, and the appearance of the adult expected to emerge.

At the appropriate time, observe the young adults and their activities in emerging, crawling on the branches and twigs provided for their accommodation, unfolding and spreading of their wings to dry, and, after an hour or two, their first flight. If fed sugar-water on a cotton-tipped swab mounted on the side of the emergence cage, they can be maintained for a period of 1-2 weeks, during which time the events of their entire adult lifetime can be observed at close range.

ACTIVITIES INVOLVING OBSERVATION OF SOME UNEXPECTED HAPPENINGS

Making careful and precise observations is an important process of science which students can develop through participation in activities that focus attention on the use of their senses. Activities that have multisensory appeal and which present dramatic, sometimes unexpected results, command a high level of student attention, and provide encouragement for them to rely on their sense preceptions for learning some important scientific information. They may recognize some relationship between a current observation and a previous experience, or they may be motivated to raise questions and to plan additional investigations suggested by the initial activity. It is this type of activity that is the most valuable in training students to develop and employ observational skills that are effective.

"Training-for-observation" type activities may be directed toward participation by an individual, small group, or entire class. The aim, however, should be the same: to sharpen the sense perceptions, to note details carefully, to call attention to some scientific phenomenon consistent with the student's level of interest and achievement potential, and to elicit from each an active response in the form of a descriptive or written record to be used for reference.

ACTIVITY: OBSERVING THE EFFECT PRODUCED WHEN LIGHT PASSES THROUGH DIFFERENT MATERIALS

Place a coin in the bottom of a cup or a cut-down milk carton, and position the container on a table so that the coin can be easily seen. Then lower your head until the coin is just hidden from view by the top edge of the container, as shown in Figure 2-3. While holding your head at this level, and without changing your line of sight, pour water into the container and observe closely as the coin comes into view, although actually still resting on the bottom.

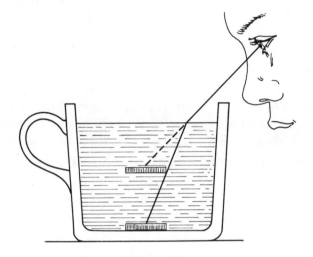

Figure 2-3.   Coin in a cup

There is an apparent displacement of the coin as it appears to rise in the water in the container. This can be related to experiences in which the water in a pond appears to be more shallow than it really is, or in which a person attempting to touch an underwater object sighted from above may miss making contact with the object because it is not actually where it is perceived to be when light rays traveling from the object to the eye pass through both air and water.

ACTIVITY: OBSERVING HOW OBJECTS ABSORB SOUND

Turn on a radio and adjust the volume to a level that permits pleasurable listening when you hold your ear approximately 15 cm. in front of the loudspeaker. Blow up a balloon

and place it in front of the radio so that it touches the loudspeaker. Put your ear against the balloon and note that the sound
can be heard as loudly and as clearly as before. Now remove the
balloon, and, in its place put a pillow of about the same thickness as the balloon. Again listen, ear to the pillow, and observe
that the sound is somewhat muffled. Then replace the pillow
with a thick book and listen once more. By comparing the way a
radio sounds when you place different objects between the
loudspeaker and your ear, you can observe the effects that
materials of different weights and densities have on the absorp-
tion of sound.

ACTIVITY: OBSERVING THE DIFFUSION OF MOLECULES

Several activities can be used to enable students to observe
the diffusion of molecules of liquids, solids, and gases.

I. Fill a glass half-full of water and add a few crystals of
    potassium permanganate. Observe the activity as the
    crystals fall to the bottom of the glass and produce a
    deep purple color. Continue to observe for a period of
    10 minutes, and note the gradual spreading of color
    from the crystals to other regions of the glass. De-
    scribe the flow of molecules of potassium permanga-
    nate and draw a diagram to show how the molecules of
    a solid become diffused in the water.

II. In one area of a classroom open a bottle of perfume,
    ammonia, clove oil, or oil of peppermint, and ask
    others present in the room to raise their hands as soon
    as they detect the odor of the substance whose identity
    has not been revealed. Note that those closer to the
    bottle generally are the first to respond and that even-
    tually everyone present can detect the odor. Describe
    the direction of flow of the molecules of the gas fumes
    from the bottle to the air in all parts of the room.

III. Moisten a piece of filter paper with phenolphthalein

indicator solution and insert it into the bottom of a large test tube or small bottle. Then hold the tube in an inverted position over the open end of a bottle of household ammonia and observe what happens. The rapid color change of the filter paper from colorless to bright red can be observed as the ammonia gas molecules flow from the bottle into the tube containing the alkaline indicator-impregnated paper.

ACTIVITY: PUTTING AN EGG THROUGH THE NECK OF A FLASK OR BOTTLE

Obtain a hard-boiled egg and a flask or bottle of the "milk bottle" design and specify those tasks to be performed by the teacher and those to be performed by a student engaging in the activity.

- Using extreme caution, the *teacher* will rinse the bottle with boiling water to warm it and then pour a small amount of boiling water into the bottle.
- After peeling a hard-boiled egg, a *student* will place it atop the open end of the milk bottle just prepared.

Watch closely as the egg is drawn into the bottle. Then describe what was observed and how it happened.

ACTIVITY: OBSERVING COLOR CHANGES WHICH OCCUR WHEN CHEMICAL SUBSTANCES ARE COMBINED

Evidence that chemicals are reacting with each other can often be detected by observable color changes. For these activities, both easily obtained common household substances and laboratory chemicals are needed. It is important that the teacher demonstrate methods for safe usage of heating devices as well as proper handling of hot water and chemicals as she prepares materials needed by students engaging in the activity. Keeping in mind these safety precautions, prepare the specific concentrations of solutions as follows:

Starch solution: Add a small amount of cold water to 1 g. of soluble starch and mix well, blending to make a smooth paste. Add this paste to 100 ml. of hot water and, with gentle heating on a hot plate, bring this solution to a boil. Allow the solution to cool before using.

Potassium iodide solution: Dissolve 1.7 g. of potassium iodide (KI) in 100 ml. of tap water.

Using the appropriate solutions and common substances indicated, perform one or both parts of the activity:

1. To a test tube containing 2 ml. of potassium iodide solution and 5 ml. of soluble starch solution, add a drop or two of a commercial laundry bleaching compound, such as Clorox. Observe what happens. Then continue to add the bleaching solution, drop-wise, until there is a second color change.

2. To a test tube containing 2 ml. of potassium iodide solution and 4 ml. of soluble starch solution, add about five drops of drugstore (3 percent) hydrogen peroxide.

Each situation is accompanied by an observable change which can be noted and described. Previous experience with the common usage of bleaching agents and with some common chemical tests, such as those used for detecting acids and bases, may inspire students to make some associations with the color changes observed.

ACTIVITIES INVOLVING
THINGS TO MAKE

Student involvement in "making things" encourages close attention to details, and, consequently, contributes to the development of good skills for observation. If the activity has sense appeal as well—that is, if it concerns something that students enjoy watching, touching, smelling, hearing, or tasting—the motivation initiated by the introduction of the activity will be sustained, with careful observations made of the intermediate steps as well as of the assembled model. For example, students who have been intimately involved in the making of a homemade fire extinguisher are able to observe its functioning from the vantage point of knowing the nature of the component parts used in its construction. The total involvement serves to sharpen the senses and to develop skills that are effective for making observations in scientific investigations.

Reporting of all observations made at all stages of this type of activity should be encouraged. It is only through practice that a student learns to describe his observations completely and accurately in what are understandable and meaningful terms, and it is only by repeated exposure that he learns to recognize those observations which are significant as they apply to a given situation.

Many make-it-yourself activities provide opportunities for students to strengthen and refine their observational skills. Among those that enhance this development are some which can be demonstrated and/or shared with others and some which provide primarily for self-learning experiences. In both, there is a strong element of attraction to the senses.

ACTIVITY: MAKING A CARTESIAN DIVER

Obtain a tall wide-mouth glass jar, a standard glass medicine dropper fitted with a rubber bulb, a piece of thin rubber sheeting or a large balloon, and a strong rubber band or length of string of the type used to tie packages.

Fill the glass jar with water. Then draw water into the medicine dropper to about a half-way mark and float it, glass end down, in the jar of water. If it does not float, release some of the water, drop-wise, until the right amount of water in the dropper allows it to float in the water in the jar.

Next, stretch the rubber sheet tightly over the mouth of the jar so as to make a taut diaphragm, and secure it with a rubber band or a piece of string so that no air is allowed to enter the jar or water to escape from it. (See Figure 2-4.)

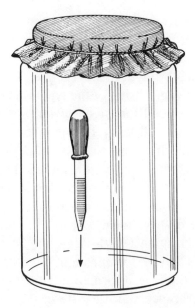

Figure 2-4.   Design for a Cartesian Diver

With the cushioned tips of three fingers of one hand, press down, gently but firmly, on the rubber diaphragm, and observe what happens to the medicine dropper. Release the pressure and continue to observe. Repeat this procedure and observe closely the level of water in the glass tube portion of the dropper. Describe what happens and consider what causes the ''diver'' to alternately dive and return to the surface.

ACTIVITY: MAKING ROCK CANDY

Emphasize the practice of *safety in science activities* by designating those tasks to be demonstrated and performed by the teacher as well as those appropriate for students to perform when engaging in this activity.

For the teacher:

> Place about 150 ml. of water in a clean glass pyrex jar or beaker and heat it to boiling on a hot plate. Add sucrose (table sugar) to the hot water until no more

sugar will dissolve. Then, carefully remove the
beaker from the hot plate.

For the student:

Tie a small weight to the end of each of several pieces
of clean white string of the type used to tie packages.
Next, suspend the piece of string from a rod, and
position the rod across the top of the beaker so that the
strings reach almost to the bottom of the beaker and
are held taut by the weights when they are immersed
in the solution. Then place the beaker in a location
where it will remain undisturbed, but available for
making observations.

Using a magnifying lens to view the details clearly, examine the crystals that are formed around the strings. Moisten a
finger, touch it to the crystal formation, and then to the tongue.
Describe the appearance and the taste of the crystals and give
reasons why this is sometimes called "rock candy."

ACTIVITY: MAKING APPLE CIDER

Obtain some ripe apples whose surfaces have been neither
waxed nor sprayed. Cut the fruit into small cubes, about 1 cm.
per side, and crush them in a food crusher or with a thoroughly
clean mortar and pestle.

Place the crushed apple bits in a large square of white
muslin cloth and squeeze out as much juice as possible, collecting it in a clean jar. Then pour the collected juice into a bottle or
a flask which can be fitted with a one-hole rubber stopper.
Prepare an outlet for the top of the flask or bottle in the following manner: insert a short length of glass tubing into a one-hole
rubber stopper, attach a fairly long length of rubber tubing to the
glass tube, and place the stopper securely into the mouth of the
flask. Then, extend the rubber tubing a distance from the flask
and place its free end into a glass of fresh water to complete the
"cider mill" assemblage.

Allow the apple juice to remain in the "cider mill" for
several days. Observe it at least once daily and check both the

flask and the jar of water for indications that a reaction is taking place. Look for signs of activity, such as the formation of small bubbles in the water and changes in the color and clarity of the apple juice. After such observations have been made, make another observation of the clear amber liquid in the flask—touch a finger to the liquid, then to the tip of the tongue, and note the taste and flavor it produces.

ACTIVITIES INVOLVING OBSERVATIONS OF LIVING ORGANISMS

Living organisms are fascinating subjects for scientific study; they are dynamic systems that have distinctive characteristics and are possessed of ingenious structures that enable them to engage in the complex processes which constitute their state of being alive.

Students really care about living things. When engaging in activities that involve living plants and animals, they are motivated to observe how the specimens are constructed and how they go about performing their life functions. When the activities involve the students themselves, there is an added impetus for making observations that are relevant. The careful observations they make may answer some of the questions they have about things that are living and may lead to an understanding of some of the wonders of life.

Although many activities of this type may suggest subsequent comparative and experimental investigations, the initial design must be simple, with the main thrust being the practice of patience while observing and the notation of observations that have significance.

ACTIVITY: MAKING A SPORE PRINT

Obtain a well-opened, firm, fresh mushroom of a field or edible variety, and separate the cap from the stipe. Position the cap, gill surface down, on a piece of white paper. Then cover the cap with a battery jar or an inverted glass dish or bowl, and allow the entire assembly to remain undisturbed until the next day. Remove the cover, carefully lift the cap, and examine the paper that was beneath it. The spores will be observed to have dropped from the gill surfaces to the paper and to have formed an outline of the gill structure and arrangement. Observe the size and color of the spores and the pattern they have formed on the paper, comparing this pattern with the undersurface of the mushroom cap.

ACTIVITY: OBSERVING GERMINATING BEAN SEEDS

Immerse 6-8 viable lima bean seeds in a disinfectant solution consisting of one part Clorox and six parts tap water. After allowing the seeds to remain for a 10-minute treatment which guards against unwanted fungal growth, rinse the seeds with clear water. Transfer the seeds to a jar of clear water and allow them to soak for 2-3 hours at room temperature. Then plant the seeds in a planting chamber that has been fashioned from an ordinary drinking glass, a white paper napkin or blotter, and a wad of absorbent cotton. Position the seeds so that they will be supported, but in clear view between the sides of the glass and the paper liner. Place the cotton in the center of the glass and add enough water to saturate the cotton and to provide a small reserve supply in the bottom of the glass as well. Then place the completed assembly (see Figure 2-5) in a warm, well-lighted area, taking care to avoid drafts, extremes of temperature, and direct sunlight. Observe daily and look for signs of sprouting, root and shoot development, and production of color pigments in the tissues.

To avoid any drying out of the developing seedling tissues, replenish the water supply as needed, and add small sticks to support any stems that have become too tall to be self-supporting in these growth conditions.

Continue daily observations and note all changes that occur. If maintained for 2-3 months, plants may become fully

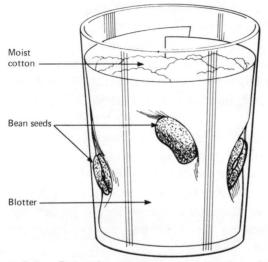

Figure 2-5. Setup for observing germination of lima bean
seeds in a glass

grown and produce blossoms that eventually develop pods and
seeds.

ACTIVITY: OBSERVING SOME VITAL
LIFE PROCESSES

I. First prepare a Ringer's solution by dissolving 0.14 g.
KC1 (potassium chloride), 6.50 g. NaC1 (sodium
chloride or table salt), 0.12 g. CaC1₂ (calcium
chloride), and 0.20 g. NaHCO₃ (sodium bicarbonate)
in 1 l. of distilled water. Then obtain an intact pair of
lungs from a freshly-killed chicken, frog, or other
small animal and keep the tissues moist with applications of the Ringer's solution both before and during
the activity. Insert a soda straw into the upper end of
the trachea and blow air into the windpipe, which
connects to the two lungs by way of the branching
bronchial tubes. Watch what happens and describe
how the lungs of an animal are alternately inflated
with air and deflated.

II. Select an aquarium fish or a tadpole for viewing and give concentrated attention to the region just behind the head. Observe closely as the flaps located here constantly move in and out. Observe more closely and locate the gills under those flaps. Note that they are red, indicating the presence of many blood vessels.

In its breathing the fish takes water containing dissolved oxygen into its mouth, passes it over the gills where the oxygen is removed and transferred to the bloodstream, and releases it through the gill covers or flaps that engage in the in-and-out activity associated with the underwater breathing mechanism.

III. Find a classmate's pulse by pressing lightly on the inside of the left wrist with the two middle fingers of the right hand, as shown in Figure 2-6. Feel the two-part pulse, as a pulsating "bump" followed by a pause repeats over and over again, several times per minute. Use a stopwatch to count the pulse beats and associate each pulsation with the rush of blood through the wrist artery after each beat of the heart.

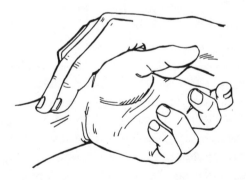

Figure 2-6.   Proper position of fingers on wrist for finding the pulse

IV. Place the bell of a physician's stethoscope a little to the left of center of a classmate's breastbone. Hold it steady and listen to the sounds which are heard through the earpieces. Describe the evenly-spaced sounds, often reported as "lub-dub, lub-dub, ..." Associate these sounds with the closing of the heart valves: the first produced by valves between the heart auricles and ventricles, the second by those between the ventricles and the arteries leading from the heart and carrying blood to all parts of the body.

ACTIVITIES THAT ARE TIMELY
FOR OCTOBER EVENTS

Activities that are timely to the season and to seasonal changes provide excellent opportunities for observation and for the development of observational skills. Many of these are typically out-of-door activities that can be scheduled for field study experiences in most north temperate regions during October. Included among them are those that involve direct observation of:

- location and identification of autumn constellations
- seasonal color changes in autumn leaves
- changes in temperature ranges, length of day, and weather patterns.

Other activities related to seasonal changes can be brought into the classroom for observation and study. Investigated here they enable students to learn how a scientist uses his senses to gather information in a laboratory situation, where he searches for a better understanding of the natural condition and the problems and questions that it poses.

Both types of activity, of course, are necessary for a science program that would have students employ the technique of observation in their studies. Those appropriate for October, therefore, must include a sampling of activities in the field and in the classroom.

Classroom instruction and practice sessions devoted to the use of star charts are needed prior to the actual observation of autumn constellations. Enlisting the aid of parents to supervise the evening event can add yet another dimension to the activity. The parental involvement in response to special requests sent home with students together with star charts and explanatory guidelines offers an opportunity for students to extend an interesting classroom activity to what can become an exciting experience linking the home and the school as viable centers of learning.

ACTIVITY: OBSERVING AUTUMN CONSTELLATIONS

On a clear autumn evening, use star charts and a pair of binoculars to locate the ''fall constellations'' that are visible in most north temperate regions in October. Facing south is generally a good position from which to spot those that travel from east to west across the southern sky.

Delphinus the Dolphin

The Dolphin is shaped like a diamond in the sky. Because of its distinctive shape and attached tail, it is easy to locate and use as a point of reference for finding other constellations on the star chart and in the autumn skies.

Piscis Austrinus the Southern Fish

Piscis represents a fish, with its brightest star *Fomalhaut* forming the great eye of the fish constellation. The fish appears to swim in the stream of water pouring from *Aquarius'* water jar. Find the Southern Fish on the star chart and look for it low on the horizon at about 9 P.M. in mid-October. It is a southern constellation that never rises more than one-fourth of the way above the horizon in most northern latitudes, so the distance it appears to travel from east to west is relatively short, with not more than 8 hours between its time of rising and its time of setting.

Pegasus the Winged Horse

Pegasus can be seen rising in the east, following *Cygnus'* bright star *Altair*. Four bright stars of this constellation form a huge square with no interior stars to offer interference with its identification when viewed in the sky.

Aquarius the Water Bearer

The stars of *Aquarius* form an irregular pattern around *Capricornus* on its north and east. *Aquarius* represents a water bearer pouring water from an urn. Its identifying feature is a wavy line of faintly twinkling stars that somewhat suggest a stream of water being poured in the direction of *Piscis* the Southern Fish.

ACTIVITY: OBSERVING THE COLORS FOUND IN AUTUMN LEAVES

Collect autumn leaves when their green color has turned to the seasonal reds, russets, browns, and yellows. Spread the leaves on a heat-resistant tray and place the tray in a heated oven. When the leaves are dry and brittle to the touch, prepare an extract: grind the dry leaves in a mortar, add acetone, and continue grinding; allow the mixture to settle for about 10 minutes; filter the mixture through several thicknesses of cheesecloth or medium coarse filter paper; and place a small amount of the filtrate, a pigment extract, in a clean glass jar.

Cut a strip of filter paper or white paper toweling about as long as the jar is high. Then using a bent paper clip inserted into a cork or rubber stopper, hook one end of the paper strip to the paper clip so that when the stopper is placed in the mouth of the jar the paper strip will hang freely, dipping slightly into the extract but without touching either the bottom or the sides of the jar. (See Figure 2-7.)

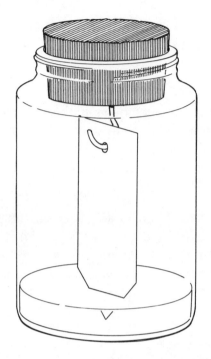

Figure 2-7.   Setup for paper chromatography

Watch closely as the acetone molecules in the mixture move up the paper strip, carrying molecules of the pigments with them and depositing them as color bands, according to their weight and solubility levels. Observe how many different color bands are formed and what colors are represented in the colorful autumn leaves. Then describe the activity observed and make a drawing of the color bands developed and of their relative positions on the paper strip.

ACTIVITY: OBSERVING SOME FACTORS THAT RELATE TO THE WEATHER

Place some crushed ice in the bottom of a wide-mouth jar or a beaker. Also place some water in a flask fitted with a one-hole rubber stopper with attachments: a short length of glass tubing connected to a considerably longer length of rubber tubing and a piece of tapered glass tubing at the far extremity. Then, under teacher supervision, place the flask on a hot plate and heat the water to boiling. Observe what happens in the flask and at the end of the tubing.

Continue to heat the water and direct the steam escaping from the jet at the end of the tube to the top of the beaker containing the crushed ice. Again, observe what happens and describe the familiar formation.

Observation means more than just looking. It implies a multisensory approach to learning for which skills must be developed through guidance and practice.

Activities for developing observational skills can be introduced early in the school year. They represent broad areas of science, timely to the season and the regular program of study. There are opportunities for including home and field studies as well as those for the classroom, for small group as well as for entire class participation, and for demonstration as well as for hands-on experiences for each student. The main objective is to provide training for the student in the techniques for making careful observations and, in the process, to have him develop a feeling for its employment as an approach to the study of science.

3

Activities for Developing Skills for Sorting and Classifying

There is a sense of order in all science. It is reflected in the arrangement of the basic building materials of which all things are made, in the natural cycling and recycling of reusable substances, in energy transformations, in the interrelationships that exist between organisms at various levels, in the distribution of living things on earth, and in the relationships between living things and their environment. The line between what comprises a condition of balance or imbalance and the ensuing order or disorder of a system or any of its component parts is often very fine indeed.

The enormity of the study of science also requires that the associated knowledge and information be placed in an orderly arrangement and that systems be devised for their expeditious handling. Consequently, the methods used in the study of science proceed in an orderly fashion; techniques are devised for sorting out, cataloging, and classifying things into related groups, tests are designed for identifying substances by their distinguishing characteristics, and skills of observation are practiced for recognizing familiar and/or recurring patterns. In effect, we look to some ordered system for the convenience of making a fast identification as well as for assistance in understanding some of the many facets of the natural world.

Science activities at the elementary level represent a wide array of topics from which students develop an awareness of the broad scope of science. Additionally, through repeated practice in the use of skills for careful observations, they come to recognize the details of likenesses and differences they witness, and to be alert to changes that occur. It is important at this point—before students get to thinking of these exposures as separate, isolated, and unrelated in any way—to plan activities that will encourage their curiosity and enthusiasm for investigating the *order* of things in science and of some of the orderly ways of the scientific endeavor.

Guiding Principles for Planning
November Activities

The main purpose of activities for developing skills for sorting and classifying events and information is two-fold:

1. to provide students with opportunities to discover the natural order of things and the influence of forces with which they interact, and
2. to introduce man-made schemes for orderly studies in science, with provisions for practice in their use and for the development of an understanding of their basic design and application.

Each activity, of course, must be approached on a personal level that puts the student directly in contact with a specific phase of science in which order in content and/or process is emphasized. A varied program of activities for the development of the desired skills necessary for practical application and for understanding the natural order of things may be planned with some attention to the following guidelines:

1. Design some activities which allow students to learn from nature and in a natural setting.
2. Develop activities at an appropriate level which afford practice in the use of established procedures for identification of materials.

3. Design activities which allow students to apply familiar procedures in a new situation.
4. Plan some activities which allow students to design their own system of *order*.
5. Plan a variety of activities which involve the biological, environmental, chemical, and physical aspects of science.
6. Provide activities which allow students to seek patterns and develop skills for organization, gradually, by repeated exposure and over a long period of personal involvement.
7. Include activities which help students to develop a familiarity with both process and approach, so that recognition of significant likenesses and differences and of evolving patterns becomes natural.
8. Provide activities which focus on relations at all levels, with application to topics within the experience of students.
9. Select activities which will promote a feeling of satisfaction and accomplishment and which will lead to making the student independent.
10. Involve students in activities which correlate with past, current, and future topics of the structured science program.
11. Plan some activities which are timely to the season and/or to other current and personal interests.
12. Include some activities which help students to organize their own experience with collections and observations or which stimulate new interests by introducing a new or unusual topic.
13. Provide some activities that present opportunities for the teacher to emphasize the importance of safety precautions to be taken in all hands-on science experiences.

ACTIVITIES FOR
PUTTING THINGS IN ORDER

Arranging an assortment of specimens into an orderly system can enhance the value of the collection to the collector. Relationships between specimens can be noted by their placement into specific groupings, and proper names can be attached to major divisions. While sorting, classifying, and naming the specimens in their collections of leaves, seashells, rocks, minerals, insects, and twigs, students are provided with opportunities for practicing skills for recognition upon which workable groupings can be based. Sorting the specimens focuses attention upon the specimens themselves and upon the need for standards in talking about them.

Elementary school students are born collectors. Using specimens collected while on a field trip or a summer vacation, or collected specifically for an activity devoted to classification, they become involved in the practical aspects of using classification keys: sorting a collection of related objects, recognizing similarities and differences, and identifying and naming unknown specimens in the collection. The activity encourages students to look closely at the characteristics of the specimens collected, to establish their own ways of comparing them, to agree upon common standards for identifying and classifying things, and to find possibilities in their own collections. The activity is a natural extension of some of the skills already established in previous activities—skills for observation—with added attention to details which are significant and to skills for making accurate descriptions that enable them to bring order and organization to an otherwise undistinguished assortment of things.

An introduction to the identification and grouping of other substances can also be applied. The employment of simple tests for common foods reveals the characteristics which serve to link together some foods and show relationships between others in the group. Similarly, appropriate tests can be performed to categorize some well-known chemical substances.

Identifying likenesses and differences can also serve as the basis for the construction of student-designed classification systems. Activities in which a student learns to use a classification system with an understanding of its design and operation are meaningful experiences. The sense of accomplishment and pleasure that they provide contribute to his growing sense of independence as he learns that he can work—and learn—on his own.

ACTIVITY: FINDING PATTERNS IN FINGERPRINTS

Working in groups of six students, make thumbprints of each member of the team, using the following procedure:

1. With the forearm resting on the desk, place the outside edge of the right thumb on a fairly-dry black ink pad.
2. Gently roll the thumb over the ink pad in a left to right direction.
3. Repeat this same roll of the thumb on white paper to produce a clear, not-too-heavy thumbprint.
4. As specified, in a prearranged code using colors, numbers, or initials, mark the back of each paper to indicate the student to whom the thumbprint belongs.

If possible, make duplicates of each thumbprint so that one team can exchange a set of prints with another, thus yielding a larger number of prints for each to examine.

Place all prints where everyone in the group can examine them, both with and without the use of a hand lens for magnification. Examine all prints, noting the size and shape of ridges, direction and number of swirls, and other details that point out likenesses and differences. Then, sort the prints into categories, as determined by their characteristics, and make a list of the factors that were used for the classification. Examine the prints closely to see if any two individuals have *identical* thumbprints.

Carefully sort through the collection to determine in what ways yours is unlike any other in the assortment, and finally, after shuffling the print cards, see if you can pick yours from among all others, based on these characteristics.

ACTIVITY: SORTING COMMON MATERIALS INTO CHEMICAL GROUPINGS

Obtain a variety of common substances to be arranged into categories according to a chemical property that can be determined by a visible color change which they bring about: a *blue-to-red* color change is produced by an acid, and a *red-to-blue* color change by a base when brought into contact with litmus paper.

Position a strip of red and a strip of blue litmus paper, 2 cm. apart, on a clean glass plate. Using a small glass applicator rod and fresh test papers for each test, transfer to each strip a small amount of each of the following substances: vinegar, saliva, lemon juice, pineapple juice, apple juice, distilled water, tap water, pond water, ammonia, household window cleaner solution, limewater, water into which you have exhaled your breath through a drinking straw, moistened crushed pine needles, baking powder in water, club soda, soapy dishwater, aquarium water, clorox solution, and a solution of carbolic soap. Other substances may be tested also.

Record the reaction—ACIDIC or BASIC—of each substance tested, individually, and note the usefulness of this test for identifying a fundamental likeness or difference that exists between common chemical substances and for classifying them.

ACTIVITY: CLASSIFYING MINERALS BY THEIR DEGREE OF HARDNESS

Collect a number of different mineral specimens and assign a number or code to each. Test each specimen by trying to scratch the surface with the following: a fingernail, a copper penny, a steel nail, and a glass plate. Then rate each specimen according to its relative degree of hardness, using the following rating scale:

Class 1—	SOFT—	Minerals that can be scratched with a fingernail
Class 2—	MEDIUM— SOFT	Minerals that can be scratched with a copper penny but not with a fingernail
Class 3—	MEDIUM— HARD	Minerals that can be scratched with a steel nail but not with a copper penny or a fingernail
Class 4—	HARD—	Minerals that cannot be scratched by any of the agents used, but will indeed scratch the glass

Using a mineral identifier, identify the minerals by name and note which are classified into each of the HARDNESS groups. Then attach a small label to each specimen, indicating its name and degree of hardness.

ACTIVITY: CONSTRUCTING A KEY FOR THE
                 IDENTIFICATION OF A
                 COLLECTION OF WINTER TWIGS

After the leaves have fallen from trees in the area, collect an assortment of twigs representing the common species. Select those twigs that show well-formed buds and, using a sharp knife, cut off specimens of about 20-25 cm. in length. For reference, attach a tag indicating, in coded fashion, the identification of the tree from which each specimen was taken. Then prepare a *Key* for the identification of the twigs, similar in design to the identification key for animals in a terrarium shown in Figure 3-1.

Guidelines for the Preparation
of an Identification Key

Examine all twigs in the collection and describe each completely as to its buds, leaf scars, bark, lenticels, and other

1A	Animal has legs	2
1B	Animal has no legs	3
2A	Animal has 2 pr. legs	4
2B	Animal has more than 2 pr. legs	5
3A	Animal body is soft, flexible, and elongated	earthworm
3B	Animal body is covered and protected by a hard shell	snail
4A	Animal body is elongated and a tail is present	6
4B	Animal body is compact, with no tail present	frog
5A	There are 1 pr. of legs per body segment ..	centipede
5B	There are 3 prs. of legs attached to body ..	ant
6A	The body is covered with scales	lizard
6B	The body is smooth and lacks scales	salamander

Figure 3-1. Key for the Identification of Animals in a Classroom Terrarium

observable characteristics. Then select one broad general characteristic that can be used to separate the collection into two main groups, and describe this characteristic as it is or is not expressed by the specimens. Working with one of the two groups, find a more specific characteristic, the presence or absence of which will further divide the specimens into two subgroups, while supplying another clue to the identification of the specimens. Continue subdividing the collection, each time giving two choices concerning a more specific characteristic, such that the appropriate choice from each pair of statements will lead to another clue and, finally, to an identification of the specimen exhibiting the characteristics. In a similar manner, subdivide the second main group until identifications of all specimens in the collection have been determined.

To test the workability of your *Key*, have a classmate select at random a twig from your collection and, using the clues from your *Key* only, make an accurate identification of the species.

ACTION-ORIENTED ACTIVITIES

Students find that involvement in action-oriented activities is an exciting phase of elementary science. Through practice in the actual employment of some simple techniques and procedures they are able to investigate the ordered arrangement of some specific materials, to identify some of the major components of various substances, and to gain some insight into how man is able to duplicate some common substances. In other "action-type" activities, students can direct their attention to change: a dynamic system interacts with certain forces and makes appropriate adjustments to maintain a state of order; energy is converted from one form to another; and changes in the physical state of matter proceed along ordered pathways.

The limiting of topics to those within the realm of student interests and experiences, both in and out of the classroom, allows for emphasis to be placed upon various approaches that focus on the order of things. In association with these activities, students gain a familiarity with both process and content. This may be reflected in their later studies in which they can be expected to approach renewed acquaintances with the *order* of things in other settings with recognition and some degree of understanding.

ACTIVITY: SEPARATING SALT FROM WATER

After examining the crystal formation of table salt, place 10 ml. of the substance in a glass, one-fourth full of water. Allow the salt to dissolve completely, then pour the contents of the glass into a shallow dish or saucer. Place the saucer, uncovered, in a warm place, and allow it to remain undisturbed.

The next day examine the contents of the saucer to determine which of the two substances, combined on the previous day, has escaped and which remains, relatively unchanged, in the saucer.

ACTIVITY: FINDING COLOR PATTERNS IN
FOOD COLORING SUBSTANCES

Cut four strips of white paper toweling or filter paper, each measuring 2 cm. wide and about 20 cm. long. Tape one end of each strip to a pencil, at intervals of about 2 cm., and trim off the opposite ends so that each strip will reach to within 2 cm. of the bottom of a wide-mouth jar. Lightly mark a pencil line 1 cm. from the free end of each strip. Then, using a toothpick for the transfer, place a small dot of red food coloring in the center of the line on one of the strips. Allowing the substance to dry after each application, intensify the color to produce a concentrated spot of red color. Similarly, using separate toothpicks, prepare concentrated spots of blue, green, and yellow food coloring on the remaining three paper strips and allow all to dry thoroughly.

Place water in the jar to a depth of 1 cm. and position the pencil across the rim, allowing each strip to hang freely into the jar with its end dipping into the water but keeping its color spot above the surface.

Observe as the water rises along each paper strip, passing through the color spots as it travels upward. When the paper strips are wet to within 3-4 cm. of the top, carefully remove the pencil and support it where the paper strips can dry thoroughly.

When dry, examine the patterns produced by each of the food colors and make a record of the color bands present and of the order in which they appear to have been separated from each of the original food coloring substances.

ACTIVITY: MAKING WHITE LIGHT BY
MIXING COLORED LIGHTS

I. Obtain three flashlights which will produce small spots of light when flashed on a screen and squares of cellophane in red, blue, and green. Cover the head of one flashlight with red cellophane, making certain that the excess is folded over the edges and held securely in place by a tight rubber band. In a similar manner, cover the second flashlight with blue cellophane and the third with green.

In a darkened room, shine spots of color from each flashlight on a white screen. Keeping the flashlights at equal distances from the screen so that the spots will be of the same size, try different combinations of colors, two at a time: red and blue to produce purple, red and green to produce yellow, and blue and green to produce peacock blue. Then try all three colors—red, blue, and green—together to produce a spot of white light.

II. Divide the surface of a toy top into seven (or a multiple of seven) equal sections. Then color each division of a seven-band section with a different color of the spectrum—violet, indigo, blue, green, yellow, orange, and red—repeating the same sequence again and again for as many groups of seven colors as the top will accommodate. Finally, spin the top and note how the colors blend.

ACTIVITY: FINDING A RAINBOW OF COLORS IN WHITE LIGHT

With a razor blade, cut a narrow slit, about 3-4 mm. wide, in a piece of dark construction paper. Place the paper over the end of a flashlight so that the light will shine through the slit only. Then fold the edges of the paper over the head of the flashlight and fasten it securely in position by taping the turned-down edges around the flashlight.

In a darkened room place a triangular prism in the beam of light from the flashlight. Move the prism until the light passing through it produces a rainbow of colors on a screen, wall, or piece of white paper. Study the path of light as it passes from the flashlight, through the prism, to the screen. Examine the color bands that result and identify the colors—violet, indigo, blue, green, yellow, orange, and red—and the order in which they appear in the visible spectrum produced when white light is separated into its components.

ACTIVITY: USING THE SUN'S RAYS
TO BURN PAPER

Obtain a hand lens or a reading glass with a fairly large double convex lens and a 2-4 cm. handle. On a sunny day set a piece of paper on a rock or paved area and hold the lens above the paper so that sunlight passing through the lens will fall on the paper. Adjust the distance between the lens and the paper until you find the distance at which all of the light rays come to a focus at the same spot on the paper. (See Figure 3-2.) Hold the lens in this position for a few minutes and observe that a hole will be burned in the paper at this spot and that the fire may spread to other parts of the paper as well.

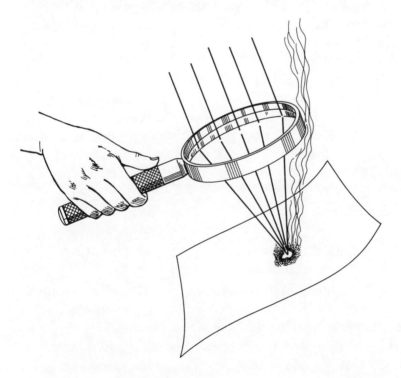

Figure 3-2.   Burning a hole in paper by concentrating light rays

Always practice extreme caution when concentrating the sun's rays: in making a picture of the scorching hot sun on the paper enough heat is produced to burn many combustible materials, including skin and other delicate living tissues.

ACTIVITY: DISCOVERING HOW FLIES MAKE ADJUSTMENTS TO TEMPERATURE DIFFERENCES

Temporarily immobilize a group of houseflies or fruitflies being reared in an insect cage by placing them in a large covered jar and submerging the jar in ice water for about 5 minutes. Then transfer several specimens to a narrow-neck bottle and attach a second bottle by taping the two together at their open ends. After the flies have revived, allow them to pass freely across the constricted areas from one bottle to the other in unrestricted flight.

On a cold day, rest the bottles on a windowsill with the window closed midway between the two bottles so that one bottle is outside the window while the other remains in the classroom. Observe the activity of the flies and determine what adjustments they make in the direction and pattern of their flight, still physically unrestricted between the connecting bottles.

ACTIVITIES FOR OBSERVING STRUCTURE/FUNCTION RELATIONSHIPS

The interest that students express in living organisms opens the door to activities that explore the relationships that exist between specific structures and the functions they perform. The design of the structures viewed in insects collected, in observations of the activities of assorted specimens in the classroom aquaria and terraria, and in the variety of ways in which students come to perceive the mechanics of their own bodies make for stimulating activities. As specific structure/function relations become focal points for consideration, students become increasingly aware of the importance of the structure/function relationship to the success of the organisms viewed in their natural setting as well as of the specimens brought into the classroom specifically for this type of activity.

Engaging in activities of this type provides students with a basis upon which to develop two important concepts:

1. The structure/function relation is observable in an ordered system.
2. Organization and adaptability are crucial to the organism's success.

ACTIVITY: OBSERVING THE SEQUENCE OF LEG MOVEMENTS AS ANIMALS WALK

I. Place a small turtle on a flat surface and allow it to remain undisturbed for a short period of time. When it begins to move forward, notice that its body remains perfectly balanced although all four legs are not used for support at all times.

Determine that all four legs are operational while walking. On paper, draw a sketch of a turtle and assign numbers to the legs: 1: front left; 2: front right; 3: back left; and 4: back right. Then observe the action of the four legs while engaging in forward motion and record the sequence of the leg movements as they are lifted one at a time. Allow the turtle to walk for several minutes while you determine the consistency of the pattern of leg movements while walking. Compare this sequence with the walking patterns of other four-legged animals (dog, salamander, cat, horse, etc.) and with the way that a baby crawls "on all fours."

II. Place a cage or a jar containing some cockroaches, beetles, or other suitable insects, in a refrigerator and allow it to chill for 10-15 minutes, or until the specimens are sufficiently immobilized for safe and easy handling. Transfer the specimens to a large glass jar or terrarium, with a cover readily available for quick placement on the top in case of an unplanned "escape" attempt.

As a specimen warms and becomes somewhat active, gently prod it to climb up a stick being held at an angle within the jar. Turn the stick to provide a clear view of the activity of the six legs used in walking. Notice how the body balance is maintained by a tripod support system in which three legs operating in unison achieve a three-point balance. Determine which legs operate in unison and the sequence of movements of the legs as the insect maintains its balance while walking or running.

ACTIVITY: DISCOVERING WHAT HAPPENS WHEN BIRDS PREEN THEIR FEATHERS

Collect some feathers from a pigeon, canary, duck, or other bird, noting the body location from which the different kinds of feathers have been gathered. Then separate the feathers into two groups: (1) the soft, fluffy down feathers that are used for warmth and insulation, and (2) the quill-type feathers that act to streamline the bird and enable it to engage in flight.

Select a quill feather and examine its structure. Note that the central shaft branches to both sides, forming the broad vane of the feather. Use a magnifying lens to examine the details of structure of a portion of the vane: rows of barbs tightly hooked together by small spines (barbules) that extend from the adjoining barbs.

Determine how the barbs can be separated and interlocked again: stroke the feather from tip to base, pushing the barbules in all directions and disrupting the interlocking mechanism; then stroke it in the opposite direction and restore its interlocked condition. Birds can be observed rehooking their barbules while preening their feathers with their beaks—in this way they reorganize disturbed and ruffled feathers into the form of strong, wind-resistant surfaces that are necessary for flight.

ACTIVITY: MAPPING TASTE AREAS OF THE TONGUE

Dissolve a small amount of sugar in water to produce a

concentration of about 5 percent. Similarly prepare solutions of table salt, vinegar, and quinine water.

Have your partner, whose tongue you will be mapping, rinse his mouth with clear water. Without revealing to him the order in which you will apply the solutions to his tongue, have him hold out his tongue while you touch it in various locations—tip, side edges, center, and back—with a clean Q-tip that has been dipped in the sugar solution. Using a designated color or symbol, record on a prepared paper diagram of a tongue the locations where he reports having detected a "sweet" taste. In a similar manner test and record the areas where he detects "salty," "sour," and "bitter" tastes. Take precautions to (1) use a different color or symbol for each test substance recorded, (2) record the code for reference, (3) have your partner rinse his mouth before each new substance is tested, and (4) use a clean Q-tip for each different solution.

Examine the color or symbol distribution on the tongue map and from it determine the areas of the tongue where taste buds for each of the four taste sensations are most heavily concentrated.

ACTIVITY: OBSERVING A COCKROACH CIRCUS PERFORMER

Immobilize a large cockroach by placing it in a container being chilled in a refrigerator or a bucket of ice water for a period of 20-25 minutes. While the insect is immobile, attach it to the end of a strong slender stick: place a drop of glue on the back of the roach, just behind the head; place another drop close to one end of the stick; and bring the two together, allowing the glue to make a firm bond. Then, holding the stick in a horizontal position, clamp its free end to a supporting structure so that the cockroach will be suspended in a horizontal position about 20 cm. above a tabletop, as shown in Figure 3-3.

Draw a star or other design on a styrofoam ball and, as the roach revives, offer him the ball. Note that he grasps the surface

Figure 3-3. Suspended cockroach trying to walk on a
            styrofoam ball

of the ball with his feet, turning it around and around. Observe
closely and study his leg movements as he tries to walk on the
ball while his position must remain stationary. Relate this
function to a similar situation in which you have observed a
circus performer on a large ball or to a person on a treadmill.

When the study has been completed, immobilize the roach
once more, and snip the glued area of the stick, thus freeing the
insect in an unharmed condition.

ACTIVITIES FOR OBSERVING ORDER
IN THE NATURAL WORLD

Activities for discovering order in the natural world de-
pend largely upon student opportunities for exposure to a wide
variety of experiences. The students have already, of course,
gained some familiarity with orderly sequences and they recognize progression and repeating patterns: night follows day;

seasons progress in a sequence of spring, summer, autumn, and winter (only to be repeated anew); a pet dog passes through several stages while progressing from puppyhood to full-grown age and size; and there is a pattern wherein the growth of plants to produce seeds alternates with the production of more plants from the germination of the seeds. Somewhere there is a recognition of the order of things observed by students which can be expanded by additional activities related to other phases of their scientific studies.

Activities that focus on how the order of things can be detected, on food and energy cycles in nature, and on the distribution, use, and reuse of earth materials stimulate student interest in what order exists in the natural world, how the order of things can be studied, what factors influence their state of order or disorder, and how these systems of order contribute to the overall balance of nature.

Some activities of this type offer students an opportunity to bring some aspect of an out-of-school activity into the classroom for further study and understanding. Many lend themselves to the longer range—started early in the month, they can continue throughout the school year—for application to other aspects of science and for recognition of patterns in an orderly system appearing in studies later in the school year.

ACTIVITY: CHECKING THE CONSTANCY OF CONSTELLATION PATTERNS

Remove one end from a rectangular cardboard box and prepare a series of individual constellation cards that can be fitted over the open end. From one piece of sturdy dark-colored construction paper of suitable size, prepare a card for the constellation *Orion*. Using a star chart as a guide, draw an outline on the construction paper, marking clearly the positions of the biggest and the brightest stars. Then punch out holes in the paper where these stars are located. Similarly make separate cards for other constellations visible in November. (*Pegasus, Andromeda, Pisces, Taurus,* and the *Pleiades* are also visible in most northern latitudes at this time of the year.)

When the cards have been prepared, view them individually. Place an electric light bulb in the box, position a card over the open end of the box, and, in a darkened room, view the pattern of stars in the constellation. Use the cards interchangeably in the constellarium for reference when locating and identifying the constellations in the night sky and when checking the constancy of their patterns when viewed on various evenings during the month and at various viewing times when conditions are suitable on a clear night.

ACTIVITY: CHECKING THE ORDER OF A SOIL PROFILE

Locate good sources of sand, gravel, clay, and rich garden soil or loam, and, using separate containers for each, collect samples to be brought into the classroom. Transfer 250 ml. of sand, 250 ml. of gravel, 325 ml. of clay, and 175 ml. of loam to a large glass jar, keeping the remaining material for a reserve supply. Add water to the jar, covering the dry materials and bringing the level of contents in the jar up to the two-thirds full mark. Cover the jar tightly and shake the contents vigorously. Then, allow the jar to remain undisturbed until the well-mixed contents settle.

After settling has occurred, examine the positions of the layers of materials settled out in the jar and, using the reserve supply as a point of reference, identify the soil type making up each layer. Measure each layer and place labels on the outside of the jar indicating the name and thickness of each layer of material making up the soil profile.

ACTIVITY: TRACING THE SUN'S DAILY PATHWAY FROM MORNING TO NIGHT

In an area of subdued light, mark a piece of blueprint paper, (about 12 cm. by 15 cm. or 16 cm. by 20 cm.) to indicate opposite EAST and WEST directions. Next, orient the paper, treated side up, in a suitably-sized flat candy box with corresponding markings for direction. Place the cover on the box and, with a sharp instrument, make a small pinhole in the center of the box top. Then, on a bright sunny day, place the box, properly direction-oriented to correspond with markings, in an area of full sunlight, and allow it to remain for several hours, or, preferably, throughout the day.

Transfer the box away from the lighted area and remove the blueprint paper, placing it first in clear water until it becomes thoroughly wetted, and then on a flat surface where it can remain until completely dry.

Examine the print and observe the long narrow streak in the form of a long arc that traces the apparent daily pathway of the sun as it appears to travel from an easterly to a westerly direction across the sky.

ACTIVITY: TRACING THE PATHWAY OF WATER IN THE WATER CYCLE

In a glass container, establish a terrarium that contains green plants, a small animal such as a salamander or a turtle, and a shallow dish of water for the animal's accommodation. Cover the terrarium and place it in an area that provides suitable light and only slight temperature variations over a period of 24 hours. Observe the appearance of the inside of the glass; look for fogging or misting, accumulations of droplets of moisture, falling of ''rain'' on the terrain, and the eventual clearing of the glass surface before the sequence of events begins anew.

Record the sequence in which these events involving both condensation and evaporation occur and determine the pattern of the *water cycle*. Relate these events to temperature changes, and determine the role played by the living and the nonliving components of the cycle in the natural environment as well as in the model.

ACTIVITY: PLANTING BULBS TO BLOOM FOR CHRISTMAS

Paperwhite *Narcissus* bulbs planted in November usually take about 4-5 weeks to bloom. During the Thanksgiving weekend plant some bulbs so that they will bloom at Christmastime. Obtain bulbs that have been stored in a cool place and a watertight bowl at least 7 cm. high in which to plant them. Fill the container about two-thirds full of coarse gravel, shell fragments, or pebbles, and place the bulbs, points up, on top of the planting medium as close as possible without touching each other or the side of the bowl. Add just enough water to cover about 1 cm. of the base of the bulbs and place the bowl in a brightly lighted area. Maintain the temperature at 13-18° C. and add water as needed, taking care not to allow the bulbs to dry out or cause them to rot because of total submersion.

Maintain the plants and observe them during their flowering period of more than a full week during the Christmas season.

ACTIVITY: FINDING SYMMETRY IN CRYSTALS

Examine several crystals of table salt (NaCl) under a stereoscope magnifier that will produce images at least 3 times larger than the specimens being viewed. Observe the shape of the salt crystals and make a metallic gift-wrapping-paper model of this type of crystal, following the pattern shown in Figure 3-4. Measure all sides carefully so that the model will be a cube. When the pattern has been transferred to paper, cut on the solid lines, fold on the dotted lines, tuck in the flaps, and tape all edges securely, so that the finished model shows the shiny surface of the paper on the outside.

Compare the shape of the model with the shape of the salt crystals observed. Then collect and examine a variety of mineral crystals found in nature and study their forms and symmetry. For each different pattern of symmetry, design and build a crystal model to represent the original accurately.

When students engage in a variety of activities involving the natural order of things, they develop important skills for use in scientific investigations. Through first-hand experiences in the identification of ordered systems in both the living and the

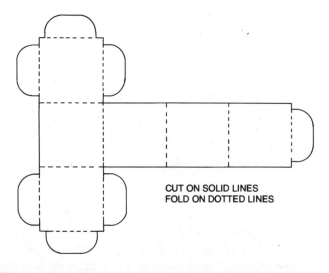

Figure 3-4. Pattern for making model of cuboidal salt crystal

nonliving worlds and in the employment of methods for arranging things into man-made systems with a semblance of order, they are helped in their continuing development of an awareness and appreciation of the broad scope of science and of an *order* that permeates the overall scheme of things.

4

Activities for Collecting, Analyzing, and Interpreting Data

Science activities that allow elementary school students a certain freedom to explore and investigate a variety of things strengthen their interest in the world of science in two important ways:

1. The satisfaction they derive from the activity may develop into a sustained interest in the topic or the study.
2. The more students learn, the more they are stimulated to find out still more.

The questions that students raise, based on a thoughtful observation, may stimulate interest that prompts them to pursue a more in-depth investigation or an on-going study of the topic. But many of their questions cannot be answered on the basis of a single observation; record-keeping of data collected may be required, sometimes over a period of time, for careful analysis and interpretation that will uncover information to be used to answer some pertinent questions or identify some significant patterns from which predictions can be made.

Activities which provide a rich and well-rounded background in stimulating science topics can be planned that will enable students to develop the necessary skills for collecting, recording, analyzing, and interpreting data. It is through this development that students gain confidence in their own ability to attach some meaning to observations that they make and to data that they collect. They are also helped to approach problems intelligently and scientifically by gaining a familiarity with an important process of science. In effect, experiencing success with the employment of these skills becomes a primary accomplishment which further stimulates interest in relying on the process of science to satisfy their curiosity and to supply some answers to their questions and problems.

Developing Skills for Collecting and Processing Data

Activities involving meaningful studies and covering a wide range of stimulating topics are needed for the development of skills for collecting, recording, analyzing, and interpreting data. Action-oriented, they are most effective when introduced as a natural follow-up of some previous activities in which students have gained experience in the identification and recognition of relationships and patterns based on close and careful observations. Thus they may be emphasized appropriately during December, when factors associated with changes in the season as well as adaptations and extensions of some studies which correlate with those in the structured course of study lend themselves to the collection and recording of accumulated information. Organized and presented in the form of graphs, charts, diagrams, drawings, and word descriptions, these data further implement the skills for careful observations practiced earlier—they may now be viewed from the vantage point of an overall analysis and interpretation as they apply, meaningfully, to the broad aspects of a topic under study.

ACTIVITIES INVOLVING DATA FROM MEASUREMENTS

The purpose of observations made is often meaningful only in the larger context of an on-going study over a prescribed period of time. For example, individual daily measurements of plants growing in the classroom become significant when viewed in relation to each other and as parts of the entire growth accomplished during the designated period. Careful examination and study of the collected data, effectively arranged in graphic or pictorial form, lend encouragement to students to find some pertinent—often multiple—answers to their questions.

The exploratory nature of open-ended investigations in both the biological and physical phases of elementary science enriches the program by providing many opportunities for student exposure to the employment of important skills for handling data. Through a wide variety of activities for this experience, students tend to become comfortable with their newfound skills and are motivated to apply them to other situations in which similar investigative procedures are involved.

ACTIVITY: TIMING A "SNAIL'S PACE"

Prepare a snail "race course" by drawing concentric circles on a sheet of white paper. Construct the outermost circle with a radius of 60 mm., and keep a uniform distance of 5 mm. between the concentric rings.

Place the race course under the flat bottom of a clear glass bowl so that the circles can be seen clearly through the glass. Then place a live snail in the bowl, just over the center of the smallest circle. If necessary use some bits of lettuce to encourage the specimen to show activity, and when it begins to move, allow it to reach a starting point such as the edge of the first circle. Then carefully time its speed as it travels over the course from innermost circle toward the outside edge, taking readings to the nearest 5-mm. distance covered.

Allow the snail to repeat the race several times and record the distance traveled for each trial. Then, calculate its average speed in terms of the number of millimeters traveled per minute and describe what is meant by a "snail's pace."

ACTIVITY: CHARTING THE GROWTH RATE OF
DIFFERENT LEAF SECTIONS

Select a young bean plant that has been grown from seed in the classroom and that appears to be growing vigorously. Next, using a plant marker grid stamp and a waterproof ink pad, carefully stamp an imprint of the grid on the leaf blades, as shown in Figure 4-1. If a stamp is not available, use India ink and a fine brush to mark off the upper surface of a leaf, subdividing it into small squares, each measuring 5 mm. per side.

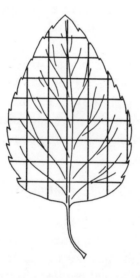

Figure 4-1.   Squares marked on surface of leaf for study of differential growth rates

On white paper make a drawing of each leaf so marked and assign numbers to those squares—usually those at the corners and in the center—selected for study. Record the initial measurements for each of the numbered squares for day one, keeping the drawing for reference to identify the squares to be measured. Then allow the plant to engage in its normal growth and maintain in chart form a record of the daily measurements of each square included in the study.

Examine the recorded data and determine, by reference to the diagram, those leaf areas which are growing at the fastest and those which are growing at the slowest rates.

ACTIVITY: MAPPING ISOTHERMS IN A CLASSROOM

After taking careful measurements of the classroom, make a scale drawing of its floor plan on graph paper. Then, using a room thermometer, measure the temperature of the air at waist level at various locations in the room. Be sure to have all sections of the room represented, and record each temperature reading in degrees Celsius in a position on the floor plan corresponding to the location in the room at which the reading was taken.

Place a sheet of clear plastic over the floor plan and draw lines connecting all points having the same temperature. After all isotherms have been drawn, examine the temperature distribution in relation to the physical features of the room and determine why all areas within the room are not at exactly the same temperature.

ACTIVITY: GRAPHING ANIMAL GROWTH CURVES

Obtain some laboratory mice for study in the classroom or at home and, when newborn mice are produced, record the birth date. Select one of the newborn mice and determine its weight in grams on day one and at regular intervals, such as every day or every other day. If several of the litter or the entire litter is weighed, calculate the average weight. Plot each day's weight on a graph and draw straight lines connecting the points for each successive date.

Continue plotting weights over a period of several weeks. Then, examine the graph and determine if the weight gain is uniform or if the early growth rate begins to taper off as the animals approach and reach maturity.

ACTIVITY: RELATING SHRINKAGE TO EARLY MOUNTAIN FORMATION

Using a metric weighing scale and a tape measure, determine the weight and the greatest distance around a firm apple.

Record this information—weight to the nearest gram and distance to the nearest millimeter—and place the apple on an open shelf at room temperature.

Next, prepare a graph for plotting the measurements taken: mark off appropriate weight units on the vertical axis to the left, distance units vertically on the right, and enough units on the horizontal axis to accommodate measurements taken twice weekly over a period of several weeks. Using contrasting colors, plot the values for each measurement taken on the first day, and keep the graph safe and readily available for plotting future measurements.

Twice a week, each Monday and Thursday, repeat the measuring and plotting of information as before, drawing straight lines of corresponding colors to connect the points plotted for each measurement taken in time sequence. Each time measurements are taken make visual observations of the apple as well. Then, by graph analysis,

(1) account for the appearance of the apple, and
(2) relate this activity to the theory proposed for the formation of mountains during early earth formation.

ACTIVITIES THAT ARE SEASONAL

Student awareness of the changing events that are associated with the coming of winter suggests many activities for collection of data that will shed light on plant and animal behavior and on assorted environmental conditions that are related to the winter season. Calendar-oriented, these activities that focus on changes—however imperceptible they may seem—over a period of time—however short—require record-keeping for later analysis and interpretation. A month-long activity devoted to the daily determination of daylight hours, for example, takes on special meaning when it is charted in December. It permits students to find the shortest day of the year and the turning point at which the pattern reverses. It also may elicit some enthusiasm for further investigations that seek explanations and test any predictions that may have been forthcoming.

Activities of this type should allow some expression of student initiative and creativity. The insights they gain into an understanding of some of the things about which they raise questions help students to build confidence in their ability to employ this process of science successfully when seeking answers to their many questions and problems.

ACTIVITY: MAPPING A WINTER CONSTELLATION

On a clear night, locate and identify the constellation, *Orion* the Hunter. Observe the constellation each night at the same time from the same location. Make a map, using guideposts in your viewing area for points of reference, showing the location of *Orion* on each night when viewing is possible.

Examine the map and interpret the gradual change in location of the constellation from the beginning of the month to the end, even though viewed at the same time each night from the same location.

ACTIVITY: FINDING THE TEMPERATURE
AT WHICH FROGS HIBERNATE

Obtain a frog that has been maintained in the classroom and a clear plastic container with a perforated cover. Place a 2.5-cm. layer of sand in the container and add enough water to fill the container to a depth of 5 cm. When the water has cleared, place the frog in the water and cover the container. Insert a thermometer through one of the holes in the cover and allow the frog to adjust to its new environment.

Next, cover the bottom of a fish tank with crushed ice and set the plastic dish containing the frog on the ice. Pack some ice around the container, taking care to avoid obstructing your view of the frog. Then allow the frog to be quiet and undisturbed. Observe the frog's activities and determine his rate of breathing as indicated by the number of times per minute the floor of his mouth moves. Record this rate with the corresponding temperature reading. Repeat these readings at intervals, each time observing his activity—burying his head, pushing sand with his forelegs, closing his eyes—and note the temperature at which he finally becomes completely motionless.

After the frog has hibernated, place sheets of dark-colored cardboard over the tank so that one-half of the plastic container is in diffuse light. Then, carefully remove the ice surrounding the container and gradually add warm water to the tank. Observe the behavior of the frog as the temperature rises and record all pertinent information, including the temperature at which the floor of the mouth begins, once more, to pulsate. Then plot this data on a graph and analyze the phenomenon of hibernation and the relationship which exists between the temperature and the frog's rate of breathing.

ACTIVITY: OBSERVING BIRDS AT A BIRDFEEDING STATION

Obtain and clean an open mesh bag such as the kind that onions are packed in when purchased at a grocery store. Prepare food to be placed in the feed bag: knead together equal parts of mixed grain and ground suet and fashion into suet balls about 5 cm. in diameter, cut apple slices, and break dry bread into pieces. After placing the prepared food in the bag, draw a string through the top and attach a hanger to the bag by which it can be suspended from a branch of a tree or other structure that can be viewed from a classroom window.

Set up a routine for making observations of the birds visiting the feeding station: use binoculars to view the feeding station for a 30-minute period at a specific time each day. During this time count the number of birds and identify those that are attracted to the feeding station. Keep daily records and, at the end of a 3- or 4-week period, analyze the data and determine if the number of visitors increases or decreases and if the kinds of birds feeding there changes or remains the same.

ACTIVITY: MAKING A SILVER CHRISTMAS TREE

Obtain a clean glass jar about the size of a small mayonnaise jar, and fill it with water. Then, carefully, and without spilling or splashing, dissolve 1 g. of silver nitrate in the water.

Next, draw an outline of a Christmas tree about 1-2 cm. tall and, using this as a pattern, cut a foil tree from a sheet of aluminum foil. Thread a small string through the top of the foil tree and attach it to a pencil so that when the pencil is rested across the top of the jar the tree will be immersed, in an upright position, in the solution. (See Figure 4-2.)

Observe closely as the tree becomes covered with silver crystals; account for the origin of the silver.

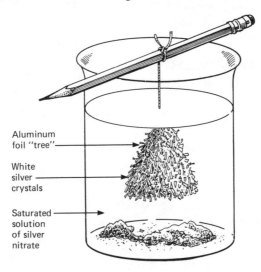

Aluminum foil "tree"

White silver crystals

Saturated solution of silver nitrate

Figure 4-2.   Setup for making a crystal Christmas tree

ACTIVITY: FINDING THE LENGTH OF A DAY

From a daily newspaper gather information concerning the time the sun rises and the time it sets each day during the month of December. From this information, calculate the length of daylight hours for each day and plot these values on a graph, drawing lines to connect values for consecutive days.

Analyze the graph and determine the pattern formed. Note the change in the length of the day from one day to the next and, for December, determine if the day lengthens or shortens and at what point there is a reversal.

ACTIVITIES INVOLVING INTERPRETATION OF DATA

Both reliable analysis and reasonable interpretation of a collection of data are predicated upon precise quantitative measurements and effective presentations that are clear and direct. How many or how few, how near or how far, how hot or how cold, how heavy or how light, how long or how short, how loud or how quiet, how light or how dark—all become important considerations that require convenient and accurate methods for careful determination, and graphs, charts, pictures, diagrams and descriptions for their recorded form.

Many varied activities involving stimulating topics attuned to the students' level of scientific performance and to the approach and content of current studies in the structured science program are effective vehicles for the development of these skills.

ACTIVITY: COUNTING STARS IN THE SKY

Obtain a tube of the type used for a roll of paper toweling and go outside on a clear night. Allow your eyes to become adjusted to the dark, and locate a place where there is no interference from artificial lighting.

Look through one end of the tube at the section of sky you can see through the other end. Count and record the number of stars viewed in that section. Then repeat the procedure, selecting several places to count and record the number of stars viewed in a total of twenty random sample areas. Add the total number of stars viewed in the twenty samples and divide this number by twenty to find the average number of stars in a sampled area. Now multiply this number by seven hundred—the estimated number of tube end samples that will cover the entire sky—to calculate the number of stars in the sky for the particular time of night when the counts were made.

In a similar manner, make star counts on different nights during the month and at different times during the same night. Then compare the star counts and interpret your findings in the light of viewing conditions, light from other celestial bodies, and other factors that might account for any differences noted.

ACTIVITY: COMPARING HEIGHTS OF BOYS AND GIRLS IN THE CLASS

Line up all of the boys in your class from the shortest to the tallest and measure their height to the nearest centimeter. Record these measurements on a chart which allows for grouping all individuals within certain height ranges, and then plot these values on a graph, connecting points plotted for consecutive height classes.

Repeat the procedure for height measurements for girls. Using a contrasting color, plot and connect points representing these values on the same axis.

Analyze the data and compare the height ranges for boys and for girls in your class, as well as identifying the average height for each sex.

ACTIVITY: FINDING DIFFERENCES IN THE LENGTH OF SEEDS

Place a handful of lima bean seeds in a bowl of water and allow them to soak for 2 hours. Then remove the seeds from the water and transfer them to paper toweling. Using a fingernail, split each seed in half along its natural seam, keeping one of the halves of each for your study and donating the other half-seeds to a classmate.

Place each half-seed, flat surface down, on top of a metric ruler and measure its longest dimension to the nearest millimeter. Construct a chart in which you record each different length class in a column where you can make a stroke count of the number of seeds in each class.

Plot the data on a graph and interpret your findings about the length of lima bean seeds.

ACTIVITY: COMPARING HEAD MEASUREMENTS

Using a 30-cm. ruler and two spring-type clothes pins, construct a head caliper with extended arms formed by tongue depressors attached to the clothes pins with tight rubber bands. (See Figure 4-3.) Place one pin against the 1-cm. mark on the ruler so that all measurements taken at the opposite end can be easily adjusted by subtracting 1 cm. from the reading.

Then, using the assembled calipers, measure the width of a classmate's head: place the ruler straight across the top center of the head, position the first tongue depressor snugly against the right side of the head just above the ear, adjust the other clothes pin along the ruler until its attached tongue depressor rests against the left side of the head, and measure the widest part of the head, rounding off to the nearest millimeter. Remember to make the adjustment necessitated by using the 1-cm. mark as a starting point. In a similar manner, measure the length of the head—the greatest length from the forehead to the center of the back of the head.

Record these values and find the *Cephalic Index* by dividing the width by the length, rounding off to two decimal places, and mutiplying by one hundred. After determining the cephalic index for several classmates, consult an anthropological system for the classification of heads. For example:

- A Cephalic Index below 77 designates a head as being LONG.
- A Cephalic Index between 77-81 designates a MEDIUM head.

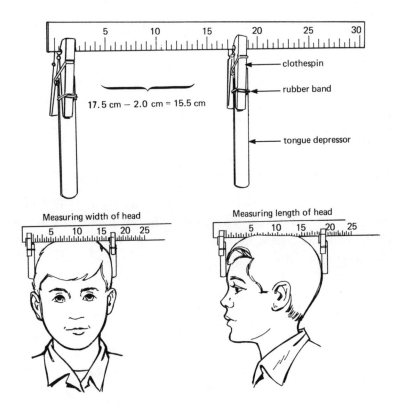

Figure 4-3. Constructing and using calipers for finding cephalic index

- A Cephalic Index above 81 designates a head as being BROAD.

Then, classify the heads measured and determine how many classmates fit into each category and whether significant differences can be noted between boys and girls or between people from different geographical origins.

ACTIVITY: FINDING THE NUMBER OF INSECTS DEVOURED BY A PITCHER PLANT

Examine some pitcher plants growing in a terrarium and select one whose older and larger ''pitchers'' are showing some signs of aging. Hold a shallow dish at the base of an older pitcher leaf and collect all of the material that is freed when a single-edged razor blade is used by the teacher to cut the pitcher at its base and separate it from the rest of the plant.

After it has been transferred to the dish, make a vertical slit in the pitcher to free all of the contents. Then, using a magnifying lens, examine the contents and identify any undigested remains of insects that have been trapped in the tubular leaf. Using fine-pointed forceps, sort out identifiable insect heads from the debris and count the number of whole heads. From this count and the average number of pitchers found on thriving plants in the terrarium, calculate the number of insects eaten by an average-sized pitcher plant and determine the need for placing insects in a terrarium in which pitcher plants are growing.

ACTIVITY: CHECKING THE CALORIC INTAKE IN FOODS PER DAY

Prepare a chart for recording the foods you eat for an entire week. First divide the chart into columns for the days of the week and list everything eaten on each day for breakfast, lunch, dinner, and between-meal snacks. Then look up and record the corresponding number of calories contained in each of the foods and add these numbers to determine the total number of calories for each day.

At the end of the week calculate the average number of calories per day and compare this number with that calculated for a classmate of about the same size and age and with that of a family member whose age, size, and activity show a difference.

ACTIVITIES INVOLVING OBSERVATIONS AND MEASUREMENTS THAT ARE RELATIVE

Interpretation of data may be distorted by information that is not based on reliable and absolute measurements. This is illustrated when students engage in activities involving situations in which observations and measurements made are *relative* and in which dynamic systems capable of making certain adjustments are employed. Data collected in this manner are often misleading and their effects upon interpretations may result in conclusions that are erroneous.

Students are enthusiastic about activities of this type. They are particularly stimulated by activities in which they are permitted to analyze situations involving themselves, while at the same time giving careful thought and consideration to the factors and conditions which exert an influence upon the data collected and their interpretation.

The inclusion of additional activities which also permit students to employ some of the manipulatory skills performed in previous activities only by the teacher allows for the development of an ever-increasing student independence in hands-on activities, with important implications for the safety factor. Performed under close supervision of the teacher, skills appropriate for the grade and maturity level of students become an important part of a science program that would emphasize total student involvement in activities where awareness of, and respect for, safety receive the highest priority.

ACTIVITY: MEASURING THE BRIGHTNESS OF AN ELECTRIC LIGHT BULB

Place an electric light bulb where it can be viewed simultaneously by two students: one who has just entered the room from bright sunlight out-of-doors and the other from a darkened room or closet. Record their responses as to the brightness of the electric light bulb.

Repeat this procedure for several pairs of classmates, recording their reactions. Then analyze the data and account for the differences reported about the brightness of the same electric light bulb.

ACTIVITY: WEIGHING OBJECTS SUBMERGED IN WATER

Obtain a spring balance, a large glass jar that is partially filled with water, and a collection of solid objects that can be submerged in the water when suspended by a string attached to the spring balance.

Tie a string around each of your objects and, taking care that they do not touch either the bottom or the sides of the jar, submerge them in the water, one at a time, and determine their weight. Then lift them out of the water and again determine the weight, this time in air.

Record each weight and account for the difference in weight of the same object in air and in water. Then describe any personal experiences you may have had when an object being lifted while under water suddenly "changed" its weight as it was lifted out of the water and into the air.

ACTIVITY: MOVEMENT OF THE MOON DURING ITS PHASE CHANGES

Consult a calendar to learn the date of the next new moon. Then, on the second night after the new moon, go outside about 1 or 2 hours after sunset and observe the moon. Make a sketch of the shape of the moon and its location with respect to the stars that are also visible at that time. Record the time of viewing on the sketch.

On the following five nights repeat the same procedure at the same viewing time: view the moon and sketch it in relation to the visible stars and/or planets. At the end of the week analyze the diagrams made and note any apparent changes that seem to be taking place in the location of the moon relative to other celestial bodies. From your collected data consider the reasons for this change and try to predict on what date the moon will be full and what its position, relative to the stars, will be on that date.

ACTIVITY: BOILING WATER BY COOLING IT

Place about 100 ml. of water in a 250 ml. flask and, under the supervision of the teacher, heat it on a hot plate until the water boils. Allow the water to boil vigorously and the steam to escape from the open neck of the flask. After the teacher has carefully removed the flask from the heat source and stoppered it securely with a one-hole rubber stopper into which a thermometer has been inserted, adjust the thermometer so that it is immersed in the boiling water. Take a temperature reading and record it as the initial temperature of the boiling water.

As the teacher offers guidance while supervising the activity, carefully invert the flask, with the water still covering the bulb of the thermometer, and support the entire assembly in an inverted position in the ring of a ring stand. Place the ring stand over a sink or basin and cool the flask by pouring a beaker of cold water over the base of the flask. Observe what happens to the water. Then take another temperature reading of the boiling water and account for the phenomenon of water boiling vigorously after a temperature drop below that of its initial boiling point.

ACTIVITIES THAT ILLUSTRATE LIMITATIONS OF SENSE-PERCEIVED OBSERVATIONS

The nature of most elementary science activities is such that students must rely heavily upon their sense perceptions for gathering pertinent information. However, the order of a system is not always directly and immediately apparent to the observer, nor do the observations always give a true picture of a situation. To be reliable, observations must be related to something that is known or to something that is being investigated—and they must be free of distortions that might lead to misinterpretations.

Students are fascinated by activities that focus attention on things that are not what they appear to be. The awareness of limitations of sense-perceived observations piques their curiosity and encourages further investigation of the phenomenon, while also providing a change-of-pace for fun and enjoyment that can be shared with family and friends.

ACTIVITY: INTERPRETING VISUAL SENSATIONS

On a white card or paper, carefully construct a copy of the ambiguous figure shown in Figure 4-4. Look intently at the drawing for 2 minutes and describe what you see. Look again and determine if you see something else. Repeat this procedure, again and again, and draw outlines of each of the figures you see in the ambiguous drawing. Then account for this visual sensation.

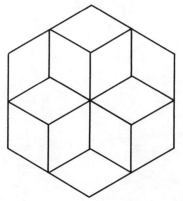

Figure 4-4.   Ambiguous figure

ACTIVITY: REPORTING TEMPERATURE CHANGES

Obtain three small buckets of equal size and place water in each to a depth that is sufficient for a classmate to immerse his hands completely. Fill the first bucket with cold water, the second with very warm water, and the third with water at room

Figure 4-5.   A sense reports temperature change rather than
a specific temperature.

temperature. Then place the three buckets on a table in front of a
classmate as shown in Figure 4-5. Ask him to immerse his left
hand into the water in the first bucket and his right hand into the
water in the second and to report on the temperature of the
water in the buckets. After he has held his hands in the designated buckets for 2 minutes, ask him to remove his hands from

the water in these buckets and to plunge them into the third bucket of water which is located between the other two. After he reports what his left hand and his right hand feel concerning the temperature of water in the third bucket, analyze the experience of each hand and account for the sensitivity of his warm and cold spots to change rather than to absolute temperatures.

ACTIVITY: SEEING A CURVED PATTERN FORMED BY STRAIGHT LINES

On a piece of ceiling tile or sturdy board, draw two straight lines, each 16 cm. long, such that they meet at one end, producing a deep V angle. Mark off each line into 1-cm. divisions and number the divisions along each line consecutively 1 to 16 toward the angle on one, and away from the angle on the other. Place pins or brads at each numbered location. Then attach some colorful string to the #1 brad and stretch the string across the angle to the #1 brad on the opposite side. Loop the string around the brad, pull it tight, and loop it around the adjoining #2 brad. Again, pull the string tight, and then work it diagonally to the #2 brad on the opposite side. Continue joining corresponding numbers on the two sides of the angle, working the numbers in sequence until all have been joined as shown in Figure 4-6. Then, pulling the string very tight, tie it in the last position worked, and cut off any excess that may remain.

Examine the curved pattern that has been formed by straight lines and account for how it was produced.

ACTIVITY: FINDING THE SHAPES OF THE MOON

Refer to a calendar or a daily newspaper to find the date of the next new moon. Begin your viewing 2 days after the appearance of the new moon and continue for a period of 14 consecutive days, which will include some daylight as well as some evening hours.

Prepare a large chart for recording observations: divide a piece of dark-colored poster paper into fourteen vertical

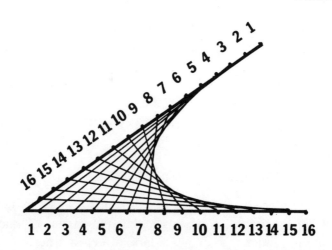

Figure 4-6.   String art uses straight lines to create a curve.

columns, one for each of the days of the study; make fourteen
2.5-cm. circles from yellow construction paper; and attach your
chart to a bulletin board.

Make one observation for each date on the chart, cutting
one of the yellow circles to represent the shape of the moon on
that date, and pasting the cut-out in its proper position on the
chart. At the end of the 2-week period examine the chart and the
various shapes that the moon appeared to take. Analyze these
shapes and account for the fact that the moon appears to change
its shape when in reality the shape of the moon remains fairly
constant.

ACTIVITY: OBSERVING STILL PICTURES
IN RAPID MOTION BLEND INTO ONE

Obtain a white card about 5 cm. square. On one side of the
card draw a birdcage and on the other a colorful parrot of
appropriate size and position to fit into the cage. Then insert the
card securely into a slit in the end of a pencil or a rounded stick,
as shown in Figure 4-7.

Place the pencil between your hands and, with a brisk
back-and-forth motion, twirl the pencil so that the card is made

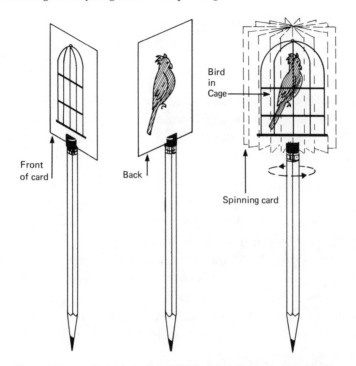

Figure 4-7. Spinning pencil with a brisk back-and-forth motion between the hands puts the bird in the cage.

to spin rapidly. Observe the effect that is produced when the card is spinning at top speed.

ACTIVITY: CREATING AN ILLUSION OF MOTION WITH STILL PICTURES

Cut white paper to make three or four dozen rectangles, each 3 cm. by 6 cm. in size. Using five of these rectangles, draw five pictures of a gull, each showing a slightly more advanced stage of motion than the one before it. The wings, for example, can be shown (1) lowered, (2) angled toward the horizontal, (3) horizontal, (4) angled upward, and (5) raised. Make sufficient numbers of each stage so as to be able to arrange them in a sequence 1,2,3,4,5,4,3,2,1,2,3, ... and to show several cycles of wing movements.

Assemble the rectangles in the desired order and, using a strong staple, fasten them together in the form of a flip booklet. Holding the booklet at the joined edge, flip the pages quickly so that, to the eyes, the pictures seem to blend into one, creating an illusion of a gull in a continuous motion of flight. Relate this phenomenon to television and to moving pictures on a screen in which a series of still pictures shown at a rapid rate produces the illusion of motion.

By engaging in activities involving the collection, analysis, and interpretation of data, students gain more than some immediate answers to questions they have about science. They also develop important attitudes concerning science as a continuing study that requires some record-keeping. The insights they gain into the process that answers some questions while stimulating them to raise still others strengthens their reliance on investigative methods in science by bolstering their self-confidence and equipping them with effective skills for learning.

JANUARY

5

Activities for Initiating Students to the Excitement and Thrill of Making Discoveries

Some of the best learning takes place when students are involved in activities wherein they experience the excitement and thrill of discovery. Finding answers to the questions students raise about topics they consider to be important is a personally satisfying experience, and the productive employment of some of their new-found science skills engenders a feeling of confidence that the processes of investigative methods can help them solve their problems. Bringing together these two motivating forces in a harmonious association provides a strong incentive for engaging in this type of learning.

Activities that allow a certain freedom to ask questions of a variety of timely topics tend to heighten the level of curiosity expressed by students. *How? Why? When? How come?* and *What for?* are among the many concerns they have for various aspects of the plant and animal worlds and for the scientific phenomena with which they come into contact on a regular—or intermittent—basis, either as outgrowths of individual observations or of a class project. The encouragement they receive to seek pertinent answers or solutions by application of previously introduced skills provides both a challenge and an opportunity to utilize *process* as well as *content* while seeking new information. Additionally, opportunities for individual input in the form of creative ideas help students to gain some insight into how facts and ideas merge when scientific knowledge is amassed and when discoveries are made.

Investigative/discovery type activities lend themselves to a broad spectrum of topics which have high student appeal and which, at this season, appropriately place emphasis on the indoor environment as a learning center. They foster an open-end approach to problem solving in which students learn to discover for themselves new information to be viewed in the light of their past experiences, their accumulated knowledge, their interests, and their involvements.

The main thrust of discovery-type activities is to provide students with exciting and rewarding experiences in the use of scientific methods for finding answers to their questions. Direct target activities that correlate specifically with the skills they are equipped to employ and with the interests and concerns they express can be grouped into several major categories.

ACTIVITIES INVESTIGATING
SCIENTIFIC PRINCIPLES AND PHENOMENA

Scientific phenomena of all types hold great attraction for elementary school students. Their questions and probing into situations involving scientific principles and concepts often suggest hands-on activities with built-in encouragement for them to investigate and look for answers on their own. Invariably the answer to one question leads to another question, and the investigation process becomes an on-going process of inquiry. By providing activities that encourage this dynamic approach to learning, much of the mystery is taken out of science, and students accept a reasonable challenge to learn to discover for themselves in topic areas of interest and in a manner they find both vigorous and exciting.

ACTIVITY: HOW MUCH CHANGE IN SIZE OCCURS WHEN A SAMPLE OF POPPING CORN IS POPPED?

Place fifteen or twenty corn kernels of popping corn in a calibrated cylinder or other measuring device for determining the volume of the corn sample in milliliters. Record the volume of the popping corn. Then pour cooking oil into a flask to just cover the bottom, and add the corn kernels. Place a loose-fitting stopper on the flask and, under the close supervision of the teacher, use a bunsen burner or an electric hot plate to apply gentle heat to the flask. While holding the flask with a pair of tongs, shake the flask occasionally until the corn kernels ''pop.''

Pour out the popped corn and again measure the sample. Then compare the two volumes—before and after popping—and suggest reasons for the change.

ACTIVITY: HOW DOES HEAT TRAVEL IN CURRENTS?

Fill an aquarium or a battery jar with cold water. Also fill a small bottle with hot water to which a drop of red ink or red food coloring has been added. Carefully insert two short lengths (each about 5 cm. long) of glass tubing into a two-hole rubber stopper and insert the stopper securely into the neck of the bottle. Lower the small bottle into the aquarium and place it in an upright position with its base resting on the bottom of the larger container.

Observe what happens and prepare a diagram to show the movement of the water in the bottle and in the aquarium.

ACTIVITY: HOW DOES HEAT TRAVEL ALONG A METAL ROD?

Obtain a metal rod, a clamp, and a ring stand that can be assembled with the rod supported horizontally about 20 cm.

above a tabletop. Tie small threads to each of six carpet tacks, and, using melted paraffin or candle wax, attach the free ends of the threads at 2.5-cm. intervals along the rod. Allow the wax to cool so that when the rod is suspended the tacks will hang downward. Then clamp the rod to the ring stand, as shown in Figure 5-1 and, under the close supervision of the teacher, use a bunsen burner or alcohol lamp to heat the free end of the rod. Observe what happens—and in what order—to the tacks, and explain the reason why.

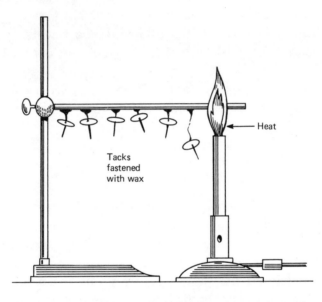

Figure 5-1.   Apply heat to end of metal rod and determine the
order in which the tacks fall off.

ACTIVITY: HOW DOES A JET OF AIR
PROPEL AN OBJECT?

Insert one end of a small plastic drinking straw into a balloon, and wrap a rubber band around the balloon and straw to band them together securely. Cut a 7.5 cm. by 12.5 cm. file card to the shape shown and make a hole about the diameter of the straw in the card. Insert the end of the straw into the hole in the card, sliding it through the opening until 2.5 cm. of its length extends beyond the hole. Then, with a second strong rubber band, fasten the balloon and straw to the card as shown in Figure 5-2.

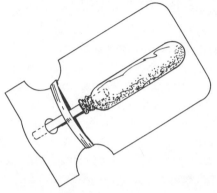

Figure 5-2.   Design for a jet-propelled vehicle

Blow air through the straw into the balloon until the balloon is filled with air. Holding one finger over the end of the straw, float the assembled vehicle upon the water in a large tub. Quickly remove your finger from the straw and observe what happens. Repeat the procedure and analyze what happens. Then give an explanation and some practical uses for this mode of propulsion.

ACTIVITY: WHAT IS THE EFFECT OF HEAT ON AIR?

Tie a string around the middle of a meter stick and attach the other end of the string to an overhead support so that the stick hangs freely when suspended. Using tape and more string, hang two paper grocery bags upside down, with one positioned on either side of the meter stick. Adjust the distances of the bags from the middle of the stick until the system becomes balanced. Then, while a teacher supervises the activity closely, place an electric hot plate several centimeters below one of the open bags. Observe what happens as the air in this bag becomes heated and creates an unbalanced condition within the system. Then describe the effect that heat has on air.

ACTIVITIES INVESTIGATING LIVING THINGS

The appeal of living things observed in the natural environment as well as those being maintained in the classroom prompt students to make inquiries and to ask questions. Students really do want to know how animals eat, learn, and defend themselves, and how plants grow, record their life histories, and yield products that are useful to man. The investigative approach to making these "discoveries" has great motivational value and places emphasis upon individual involvement in the employment of scientific processes to obtain first-hand information.

When procedures are kept simple and directly related to the target questions, activities serve to supply answers to questions raised by students and to safeguard against experiencing failure. In making the relevant "target" observations, students are helped to build confidence both in themselves and in the ways of science. Selected activities in this area contribute importantly to the development of an understanding of *how* information is discovered as well as to the actual experience of discovery itself.

ACTIVITY: HOW CAN CASTS OF ANIMAL TRACKS BE MADE AND STUDIED?

Visit a park, playground, beach, or other area on a day when the ground surface is soft and wet. After examining the area and finding some interesting footprints made by a small mammal or a bird, select a print which is sharply outlined and sunken about 1 cm. in the mud or sand. Sprinkle the print lightly with talcum powder and, using a strip of cardboard, construct a low wall (about 2 cm. high) around the print, forming the desired size, shape, and thickness for the finished cast. Then, overlap the ends of the strip and fasten them together with a paper clip.

To make a negative cast: Mix non-asbestos plaster of Paris with water, stirring briskly to make a smooth mixture with the consistency of pancake batter. Then, gently pour the wet plaster into the track, filling it to the top of the wall. Allow the cast to set and harden. After about 15 or 20 minutes, lift the cast carefully and wrap it in protective layers of tissue paper.

To make a positive cast: After the negative cast is completely dry, brush off any debris that may have become attached, and apply a coating of vaseline or other grease to its surface. Place a cardboard collar around the outside edge of the cast, using a string or an elastic band to hold it securely in place. Then pour a fresh plaster of Paris mixture into the mold. Allow this cast to dry thoroughly and to become hardened before separating the positive from the negative. Then wipe off any remaining traces of grease and examine the positive cast which shows the sunken impression of the animal's foot just as it appeared in the mud or sand.

Study the positive cast and determine the characteristics of the footprint and the identification of the animal that made it. The negative may be kept for making additional positives, if needed.

ACTIVITY: HOW LONG DOES IT TAKE FOR BABY CHICKS TO DEVELOP?

Obtain twelve fertile hens' eggs from a chicken farmer or a chick hatchery and place a pencil mark, such as an X, on one side of each egg. Place the eggs, X side up, in an egg incubator maintained at a constant temperature of 38° C. If no incubator is available, a styrofoam chest heated with a Christmas tree light bulb can be used. Also place a moist sponge or a shallow dish of water in the "incubator," and record the date for future reference.

Turn the eggs twice daily—X side up in the morning, X side down in the evening—and maintain conditions of temperature and humidity in the incubator for a period of 3 weeks. Watch for signs of chicks about to peck their way out of the shells. When the eggs hatch, transfer the baby chicks to a 38° C. brood chamber. (If necessary a brood chamber can be fashioned from an empty cardboard box or large rectangular aquarium tank heated with a Christmas tree light bulb.) Then, while their feathers are drying and the chicks are becoming stronger, check the calendar and your records to determine how much time and what conditions were necessary for the chicks to develop from the incubated fertile hens' eggs.

ACTIVITY: HOW TALL WILL BREAD MOLD GROW IF GIVEN OPTIMUM CONDITIONS?

Obtain a slice of fresh bread of a homemade or local bakery variety, a plate culture of a sporulating black bread mold, a large battery jar or glass bowl, some paper toweling, and a tray or other flat surface upon which to assemble the "garden."

Line the bottom of the tray with several thicknesses of moistened toweling and place the bread slice on top of the toweling. Use an atomizer to moisten the surface of the bread as well. Next, remove the cover from a petri dish containing a growth of sporulating bread mold and note the black spore cases adhering to its inside surface. While holding the cover about 7.5 cm. above the bread, tap the cover gently and cause the spores to become dislodged and fall in an evenly-distributed pattern onto the surface of the bread. Finally, cover the planting with an inverted glass bowl or battery jar, and place the entire assembly in a darkened closet where it can remain undisturbed at room temperature for about 4 days. Then remove the tray from the closet, but do not lift or in any way disturb the glass cover!

Observe the luxuriant growth of mold that covers the bread completely and measure the height to which it extends above the surface of the bread. Use a magnifying lens to examine the white thread-like growth and the multitude of black spore cases dotting the entire growth. Continue to observe for another 2-3 days, noting the changes in appearance and the growing abundance of spore cases during this period. Then, remove the glass cover and watch closely to see what happens to the light, fluffy, airy growth within minutes of the removal of the cover.

ACTIVITY: HOW CAN BULBS BE "FORCED" IN WINTER?

Select some good-quality bulbs of a flowering species such as *Amaryllis* or of a fancy-leaf species such as *Caladium*. Also select an attractive planter that provides for drainage, and place some pot shards or small stones over the drainage holes in its bottom. Fill the pot about halfway with a growing medium made of equal parts of potting soil, sand, and peat moss. Place the bulbs on top of the planting medium, positioning them close together without touching and with their tips not higher than the rim of the planter. Sprinkle some additional planting medium around and between the bulbs so that they are almost covered, with only the tips visible. Apply water lightly to allow settling, and add more medium if necessary. Then water thoroughly and place the container in a darkened area at a reduced temperature of about 5° C. Check the planting periodically, adding water when necessary to prevent drying out. When the buds are extended about 3 cm., move the planter to an area of subdued light and a temperature of about 15-18° C. After a few days, move them to an area at room temperature where they will receive stronger light and protection from drafts. Water the plants regularly and observe their production of colorful foliage and/or showy blooms indoors during the winter season.

ACTIVITY: WHAT RECORDS CAN BE FOUND IN THE CROSS SECTION OF A TREE TRUNK?

Locate the trunk of a large tree that has been cut down recently and examine the cut end. Note the number of light-colored and dark-colored rings appearing in the cross section and determine the age of the tree by counting the number of ''annual'' growth rings. Assuming that the outermost ring was produced during the last calendar year, count backward to determine the year in which the tree started to grow from a seed.

Next observe the thickness of the rings that represent how much growth occurred each season and determine during which years and at what age the tree had its greatest and its poorest growth. Then observe closely to see if a single ring appears to be of uniform thickness all the way around and suggest what might be indicated by the appearance of one or more rings that are thicker on one side of the tree trunk than on the other.

On the basis of your examination, make a list of all of the things you can tell about the tree and the conditions it experienced during its lifetime.

ACTIVITY: WHAT DO BARN OWLS EAT?

Search an area near old buildings or protected cliffs to locate a barn owl's roosting spot and collect some of the owl pellets which have been regurgitated and have fallen onto the dry, relatively protected surfaces below.

In the classroom, prepare to examine the contents of one of these pellets. Using forceps or tweezers, separate a pellet and carefully spread out its contents. Examine the skulls and individual bones of the prey species that have been eaten. Taking care not to damage the delicate little bones and skulls, sort out the whole skulls and identify them by comparing them with small mammal skeleton charts. Then count the number of whole skulls found in the pellet and determine the number and kind of small mammals that were eaten by the owl in one meal, as represented by one pellet. Using the estimate that an average barn owl will regurgitate two pellets per day, explain how owls control the rodent population and what part they play in a predator/prey relationship in a food chain.

ACTIVITIES INVESTIGATING
PERSONAL MATTERS

The curiosity that students have about themselves is evident in the questions they raise. It also offers strong motivation for the students to engage in activities that are designed to help them find answers to these questions.

Activities in which students investigate certain aspects of themselves provide direct and purposeful experiences which lead to the development of important concepts. For example, activities that ask questions relating to their senses reveal that many senses actually involve both *sensations* received by the sense organs and *perceptions,* or the way the brain interprets the sensations. Consequently, students are enlightened by answers that reveal the actions of their bodies to be more than those of mere "human machines" and that shed light on the differences between individuals. Each activity, focused on a stimulating target question and designed for the investigative approach to problem solving, provides opportunities for making discoveries in a new and challenging situation that has specific *personal* overtones.

ACTIVITY: HOW MANY SWEAT GLANDS ARE PRESENT
IN ONE SMALL SQUARE OF SKIN?

Dip a cotton Q-tip in a solution of 1 percent iodine and use it to paint a small area of about 2-3 sq. cm. on the forearm or the back of the hand. Gently warm the painted area for approximately 5 minutes. Then place a square (about 5 cm. per side) of Bond paper over the iodine-painted patch and hold it in place for 30 seconds.

Carefully remove the paper square from the painted skin area and examine the surface of the paper that was in contact with the skin. Measure and mark off 1 sq. cm. on the paper and count the number of blue dots appearing in this section. This number represents the number of sweat glands per square centimeter of skin exposed on this part of the body. Relate this investigation to the chemical test for starch and determine what must be present in the Bond paper to make the use of this test possible and what role was played by sweat from the sweat glands. Then plan to repeat this test on other skin areas to determine if sweat glands are distributed equally on all skin surfaces of the body or if there are some areas that are better supplied than others.

ACTIVITY: DOES YOUR EYE REALLY SEE OBJECTS UPSIDE DOWN?

Make a pinhole in the center of a 12 cm. by 16 cm. file card. With your left hand hold the card about 15 cm. in front of your face so that the hole is between your left eye and a bright bulb on the other side of the card. Then close your right eye.

Now hold a sharpened pencil in your right hand so that the pointed tip is close to your open eye and in the beam of light from the hole. Move the tip slowly up and down and observe its shadow in the hole. As the point moves up, note the direction in which the shadow moves and explain the difference between the sensations your eye receives and the way in which your brain perceives images of the objects at which you are looking.

ACTIVITY: HOW IS THE BRAIN PROTECTED AGAINST A BLOW TO THE HEAD?

Obtain a wide mouth jar with a screw cap and a block of styrofoam that will fit inside the jar with very little room to spare. Make a nail hole in the center of the jar cap. Then tie one end of a string around the block, and thread the other end through the underside of the jar cap so that it comes out at the top of the cap. Holding this end of the string, screw the cap on the jar and adjust the string so that the block dangles about 2 cm. above the bottom of the jar. Now tape the string to the outside of the jar cap.

Remove the cap and fill the jar with water. Lower the block into the water and screw the cap back into place, maintaining the distance between the block and the bottom of the jar as before. Pack modeling clay around the hole in the middle of the cap to prevent any water from leaking when the jar is turned upside down.

Now turn the jar upside down and hold it in one hand while you use the other hand to strike a gentle blow against the side of the jar. Observe what happens. Then strike the jar a harder blow.

Analyze what happens to the block (brain) when a blow is struck against the jar (head) and interpret the role of the water (fluid surrounding the brain) and the extent to which it can offer protection to the "brain" by preventing its actual contact with the skull bones of the head.

ACTIVITY: DOES VIEWING IN A MIRROR AFFECT ABILITY TO MAKE A TRACING?

Set a large rectangular mirror on edge on a desk or table with some working space in front of it. Next, set a book on edge in front of the work surface so that a person sitting at the desk cannot see this work surface, except by viewing it in the mirror.

On white paper draw an outline of a large star, and inside the star draw an identical star, 1 cm. within the perimeter of the first so that the appearance is that of a star with a double border. Place this paper on the desk. Then sit at the desk and trace a pencil line between the double outline of the star while viewing what you are doing only by looking in the mirror.

Examine your finished mirror tracing and determine how seeing a reflected image affects the direction in which your hand moves.

ACTIVITY: HOW MUCH AIR CAN BE FORCED OUT OF THE LUNGS?

Obtain a large jar having a capacity of at least 4 l. and

attach a 2.5-cm. strip of waterproof tape, vertically, to the outside wall. Next calibrate the jar: fill a 1-l. vessel with water, transfer this water to the jar, and, using a waterproof marker, mark the 1-l. level on the tape. Repeat this procedure until the jar is completely filled with water and the tape shows the capacity marked off in full and fractional liters.

Invert the filled jar in a deep pan of water, taking care to place a glass plate over the mouth of the jar until it is completely submerged, thus avoiding the inclusion of any small air bubbles. Place one end of a 62-cm. length of rubber tubing under the mouth of the jar, leaving the opposite end free for use as a mouthpiece. Then, take the deepest breath possible, hold it, and, by blowing into the tube, force as much air as possible from the lungs.

Observe the displacement of water in the jar and check the markings on the tape to determine the volume of air that was expelled from the lungs in one forced breath.

ACTIVITY: HOW FAST DO THE FINGERS REACT TO WHAT THE EYES SEE?

Obtain a meter stick and enlist the aid of a classmate to work with you.

Hold the stick vertically by the end showing the highest reading so that the opposite end, showing the zero marking, is at your partner's eye level. Have your partner place the thumb and index finger of his right hand close to but not touching the zero mark and ask him to grab the stick the moment he sees it begin to fall.

Without warning, release the stick. Then, immediately check the position of your partner's thumb on the meter stick and read the distance in centimeters that it fell before he grabbed it. Convert this distance to reaction time using the chart shown in Figure 5-3, and repeat the procedure for several trials to determine if the reaction time can be shortened by practice.

Distance of fall in cm.	Time in seconds
7	0.14
10	0.16
14	0.185
15	0.19
17	0.20
18	0.205
19	0.21
20	0.215
28	0.25
33	0.27
40	0.295

Figure 5-3.   Chart for finding reaction time from the distance in fall measured in centimeters

ACTIVITIES INVOLVING COMMON SUBSTANCES AND MATERIALS

Learning in science requires activity on the part of the learner. In many cases this implies "doing" something of a concrete and tangible nature related to a problem being investigated or a question being probed.

Student learning experiences, which usually center about indoor studies at this time of year, can be broadened and enriched by including "doing"-type activities. This allows for appropriate aspects of outdoor study to be brought into the classroom for investigation and also for topics not generally thought of as *science*. The values that are thusly derived stem primarily from the in-depth student involvement that is entailed and from the opportunities for innovative student input that are offered. Consequently, each student is permitted to experience learning on a very personal level and to develop some broad understanding of timely topics by finding answers to specific target questions.

ACTIVITY: HOW CAN PLANT SUBSTANCES BE USED TO INDICATE WHETHER A MATERIAL IS AN ACID OR A BASE?

Clean and cut a few red cabbage leaves into small pieces. Fill a glass jar one-fourth full of the pieces and add enough boiling water to fill the jar to the halfway mark. Set the jar aside and allow the cabbage pieces to soak in the hot water. Then, after 30 minutes, when the water has turned purple in color, remove and discard the pieces of cabbage, but keep the purple liquid for testing.

Using a clean medicine dropper, add white vinegar (a known acid) one drop at a time to the purple liquid until it turns from purple to a decided *red* color. Then neutralize the acid solution by the addition of ammonia, a known base. With a clean medicine dropper, add the ammonia drop-wise until the purple color, indicating a neutral state, is restored. Then continue adding ammonia and observe the color change to *blue*, and finally to *green* when the liquid becomes basic.

Based on the color changes associated with known acids and bases, use the cabbage juice indicator to classify a dissolved Alka Seltzer tablet, a dissolved aspirin tablet, a colorless laundry detergent solution, and other common substances.

ACTIVITY: HOW CAN A GLASS JAR BE TURNED INTO A MAGNIFIER?

Select some interesting objects whose details of structure are not easily detected by the naked eye and whose viewing would be enhanced by a small amount of magnification. Some easily obtained specimens and their preparation for viewing are listed below.

- Touch the cotton pad of a Q-tip, to which a drop of glue has been applied, to the wings of a captured fly.

- Mount an entire flower or one flower organ, such as the pollen-bearing anther from the center of a lily, on the pointed end of a dissecting pin or probe.
- Attach a portion of a geode to a stub by gluing one outside edge to the eraser end of a short pencil.
- Paste a jar label stating the ingredients included or a set of directions printed in very small type size to a file card.
- Mount quill or down feathers collected from a variety of available birds—chicken, pigeon, parakeet, canary, or turkey—on the pointed end of a dissecting pin.
- Mount a twig bearing a terminal bud formed in late summer on the pointed end of a dissecting pin or needle.

Next, fill a clean glass jar or small fish bowl with clear water, and, holding the object to be viewed on the side opposite, observe the specimen while looking through the glass and water. Examine the specimen closely and compare this view with the appearance of the object without the "magnifier." While passing through the glass and water, some bending of light rays occurs and results in a small amount of magnification. This enables the viewer to see small objects and their details of structure in slightly larger than actual size.

ACTIVITY: HOW CAN A CRYSTAL GARDEN BE GROWN FROM CHEMICALS?

Place 50 ml. of table salt in the bottom of a glass bowl and arrange four charcoal briquets or equivalently-sized pieces of coal, coke, or charcoal on top of the salt layer. With a medicine dropper, add a few drops of red mouthwash, mercurochrome, food coloring, or colored ink to the charcoal surfaces. Then prepare a chemical mixture composed of the following:

    100 ml. water
    50 ml. laundry bluing
    10 ml. household ammonia

Pour the chemical mixture over the charcoal, and allow the assembled materials to remain undisturbed for several days.

Using a magnifying lens, observe the crystals that develop. Maintain the ''garden'' for 3-4 weeks and note all changes as they occur over this period of time.

ACTIVITY: WHAT IS THE DESIGN OF A ONE-PIECE HANGING PLANT/PLANTER?

Obtain a fairly large fresh carrot and slice off the top about 7 cm. from its upper end. Cut off any green leaves that may be present but allow the leaf stems to remain.

From the cut end of the carrot, scoop out enough of the vegetable to form a small hollow. Using toothpicks, poke two small holes in opposite sides of the carrot piece. From these holes suspend the carrot with string or fine wire, freshly-cut side up, in a sunny window.

After hanging the carrot, fill its small hollowed-out well with water. Then check the water level daily and add more water, as needed. Observe the activity occurring at the bottom of the hanging basket and note the appearance of stems and leaves that curve gracefully upward in an amazingly attractive display. Give your all-in-one plant and planter tender loving care and it will grow luxuriantly right into its flowering stage.

ACTIVITY: HOW CAN THE GROWTH OF A VINE BE TRAINED?

Select a sweet potato which is plump and firm. Position three toothpicks equally spaced around the potato and press them part way into the fleshy tissue. By resting the toothpicks on the rim of the glass jar, support the potato above a constant water level which covers the lower portion, but never floats the whole potato. Set the jar in a cool dark place for about 10 days until a luxuriant tangle of fine roots can be observed at the base of the potato in the jar. Then transfer the actively growing plant to a deep bowl filled with pebbles and maintain the water level touching the base of the potato.

Place the bowl in a sunny window and observe the appearance of the top growth in the form of swellings that eventually become spikes. Pinch out all but two or three of the spikes, allowing those remaining to develop into leafy lines. Attach strings for them to twine their tendrils about as they grow into a lush sweet potato vine which frames the window.

ACTIVITY: CAN COOKIES BE BAKED USING A *METRIC* RECIPE?

Obtain a measuring device calibrated in milliliters and a baking pan which measures approximately 24 cm. by 33 cm. by 5 cm.

Ingredients—Carefully measure out the following:

> 120 ml. butter or margarine
> 360 ml. graham cracker crumbs
> 240 ml. chopped walnuts
> 240 ml. chocolate morsels or chips
> 320 ml. coconut flakes
> 320 ml. sweetened condensed milk

Directions: In a 24 cm. by 33 cm. by 5 cm. baking pan, melt the butter or margarine. Remove the pan from the heat and sprinkle graham cracker crumbs over the melted butter. Distribute the chocolate morsels and chopped walnuts evenly over the cracker crumbs. Add an evenly distributed layer of coconut flakes. Over all of the assembled ingredients pour the sweetened condensed milk. Bake at a temperature of 185° C. for 25 minutes or until golden brown. Then cool and cut into 7.5 cm. by 3.8 cm. bars and ENJOY!

Using an English to Metric Conversion chart, convert other favorite recipes to *metric* and treat your friends and family to other metric goodies or, for a very special occasion, to a Metric Birthday Cake.

ACTIVITY: HOW CAN SNOWFLAKES BE USED AS MODELS FOR MOBILES?

On a snowy day, place a piece of black velvet at outdoor temperature where it can be chilled to a temperature below freezing. Place the chilled velvet outside a window and capture some snowflakes by letting some crystals fall on the chilled surface. Bring them into the classroom and use a magnifying glass to examine the intricate patterns—all six-sided figures, each with a different design. Sketch the many designs observed. Then try to make some snowflake cut-outs, using white letter paper, scissors, thread, glue, and the following directions.

For each snowflake use one-half sheet of letter-size typing paper. After cutting a full sheet of paper in half lengthwise, fold one of the rectangular strips crosswise into 1-cm. accordion-style folds. Cut a notch in each long side at the center. Double a 30-cm. piece of thread and tie it around the paper notch. Then cut out symmetrical wedges on both sides of the center notch (see Figure 5-4) to copy the snowflake pattern. Apply a line of white glue along the edge of one outside fold of paper and lay the threads flat along the glue strip. Bring the two sides of the outside fold

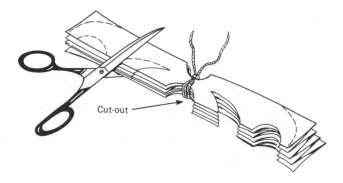

Cut-out

Figure 5-4. Snowflake pattern.

together so that the glued surfaces make contact with each other, sandwiching the threads between them. In a similar manner glue together the sides of the opposite outside fold, allowing the snowflake to open fully. Then knot the ends of the threads at one end and hang the snowflake mobile.

Students learn science as a direct result of their own activities. Through actual involvement in first-hand experiences which include both physical and mental participation, they gain important insights into the methods which may be employed for seeking and finding satisfactory answers to some questions of importance. In the process they develop positive attitudes toward science and an appreciation for the methods by which scientists discover new information.

6

Activities for Planning and Conducting Experiments

There are few things that excite elementary school students more than "experimenting." They are wildly enthusiastic about probing into all sorts of things, often improvising and manipulating as they go. Clearly they are curious and have great interest in discovering what will happen when they alter some factor or condition within a model.

The greatest satisfactions, of course, derive from experiments in which the students have done some initial planning and preparation. The students must start with a clear understanding of what they are looking for by way of an answer to a question or the solution to a problem. Then they must design procedures to test a hypothesis for something germane to the topic which seems to be true, but which they have not yet established scientifically. In the process they are afforded an opportunity to make use of their scientific skills for observation, record-keeping, analysis and interpretation of data, and making personal discoveries, as developed in previous activities. By putting it all together they gain experience with the scientific experiment—a useful process of science which develops naturally out of other forms of scientific endeavor.

The success of a scientific experiment is due primarily to two basic factors:

1. The design of the experiment.
2. The manner in which students make observations

The experimental design must recognize that students at the elementary level will require some measure of guidance, instruction, and direction, and that the observations made by the students should relate to something about which they want to know. Further, it should encourage students to think and to formulate some conclusions based on observations that have been carefully and accurately made.

Simple experiments, simply designed and appropriately adjusted for the grade and performance level of the students, are the most satisfactory. They can be developed in a series of steps which are arranged in a logical sequence, following the format below.

1. Define the problem to be investigated.
2. Collect all available information relating to the problem.
3. Form a hypothesis, based on your ideas and the available information, stating what you think is the answer to the problem.
4. Plan and perform an experiment to test the hypothesis.
5. Carefully observe and accurately record data from the experiment.
6. Draw conclusions based on the results of the experiment, and determine if these data support the hypothesis or suggest some other factors to be considered.

It is essential that there be a real purpose for planning and performing an experiment and that the students be allowed sufficient freedom to carry out the procedures with a minimum of help. Answers should not be supplied too readily, and students should be encouraged to guess and make predictions about what they think will happen. Performing the experiment will test the correctness of a prediction they have made and will supply them with a useful technique as they engage in science activities devoted to a search for meaning.

EXPERIMENTS THAT INTRODUCE STUDENTS TO IMPORTANT TOPICS IN SCIENCE

When students do not know what the results will be for the experiment they are performing, they are actively engaging in the most effective approach to scientific investigation. Rather than performing an exercise which merely confirms some information that has already been presented in a classroom situation, they become intimately involved in a true discovery experience through which they acquire a basis for understanding the principles and concepts that will be developed later in a class follow-up of the experiment. For this reason, if at all possible, students should be allowed to investigate the topic experimentally *before* it is treated as a classroom study. Basic experiments, correlated with topics for current study can be planned, with options for additional investigations included as well.

There are many topics which lend themselves to student experimentation. Questions based on observations related to air, water, fire, light, magnetism, the weather, and living things are among those that provide high student motivation for planning and conducting experiments directed toward a search for meaning. However, since most animal experimentation is too complex for elementary school students to handle, this phase of experimental work should be deferred until a later time. More appropriately, a sampling of physical science topics can be combined with studies involving plant life and some simple experiments involving the students themselves as the experimental subjects. Providing a program that includes experimental studies of this nature introduces elementary school students to many of the important topics in science.

EXPERIMENT: COMPARING SOIL TYPES

Problem: How do soil types differ in their ability to hold water?

Procedure: Obtain three identically-shaped liter jars and samples of three different soil types: sand, garden soil, and clay. Dry all soil samples thoroughly and place a sufficient amount of each in its individually designated jar to reach the half-full mark. Next add 250 ml. of water to each jar, allowing the water to run slowly into each of the soil types. Record the amount of time it takes for the water to work its way below the surface of the soil in each jar, keeping records of the time required to reach a depth of 3 cm. and 6 cm., and finally, to reach the bottom of each jar.

On the basis of the data collected, compare the drainage properties of the three soil types and suggest some advantages and disadvantages associated with the use of each.

EXPERIMENT: INVESTIGATING IMBIBITION PRESSURE

Problem: Do seeds exert pressure when they imbibe water?

Procedure: Obtain two small glass jars, such as those used for baby food, some viable dried seeds such as a lima bean or broad bean variety, and a mixture of non-asbestos plaster of Paris. Mix water with the plaster of Paris to make a thick stiff wet plaster. Place six large seeds in one jar, and pour the wet plaster into the jar, filling it completely, while stirring the mixture with a clean stick to distribute the seeds evenly throughout the plaster. Similarly, prepare the second jar of plaster, without seeds, to act as a control. Place both jars in an area where they may remain until the plaster is completely dry. Then place the two jars in an inverted position in a shallow pan of water. Allow them to remain for a period of time and note that the jar containing seeds eventually begins cracking and breaking into many pieces, while the one containing only plaster remains intact.

Relate the breaking of the glass to the pressure produced by the imbibing seeds which swell when they receive water carried to them by the porous plaster. Relate this observation also to the cracking of pavements and breaking up of rocks when seeds, having found their way into spaces and crevices in sidewalks, driveways, and large rocks, exert pressure when they imbibe water and swell during the process of germination.

EXPERIMENT: INVESTIGATING THE RELATIONSHIP BETWEEN DEPTH AND WATER PRESSURE

Problem: Is the pressure exerted by water the same at all depths?

Procedure: Use a large nail to drive three holes at different heights along the side of a large tin can or plastic jug such as a Clorox bottle. Cover the holes with a strip of masking tape, as shown in Figure 6-1. Then fill the jug with water and place it over a sink or a large tray. Quickly pull off the masking tape and observe the flow of water that streams out of the holes and into the sink. Watch closely and determine the horizontal distance to which each of the three streams squirts water. Then, on the basis of your observations, determine the relationship between depth and the pressure that is exerted by water.

EXPERIMENT: DETERMINING THE EFFECT OF SALT WATER ON LIVING TISSUE

Problem: What happens when cells not normally in contact with salt water are transferred to a saltwater environment?

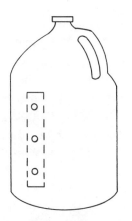

Figure 6-1.   Device for measuring downward pressure exerted by water at various depths

Procedure: Place seven raw potato slices of equal size and a
thickness of about 2 mm. in a container of tap
water. Remove one of the slices and observe its
general appearance. Also test its crispness by
bending it with your fingers. Transfer three of the
remaining slices to a similarly sized jar containing
water to which salt has been added. Then place
both jars in a cool area where they may remain
undisturbed for 24 hours.

The next day examine the potato slices from both
environments and observe their size and appearance. Test one from each environment to determine its crispness. Compare the potato slices
from the two environments. On the basis of the
information you collected, describe the effect of
salt water on living substances which are removed
from natural fresh water surroundings and placed
in a saltwater environment.

**EXPERIMENT: DETERMINING THE DIRECTION
OF PLANT ROOT GROWTH**

Problem: In what direction do plant roots grow when seeds
are planted in various positions in the soil?

Procedure: Obtain a rectangular glass or clear plastic container, such as an aquarium and a piece of cardboard of suitable size to cover one side of the container. Fill the container with a good potting soil mixture and plant a group of viable corn seeds at the recommended depth, pressing each against one of the flat sides of the container, designated "FRONT" through which they can be viewed clearly from the outside. Place the seeds carefully with their tapered ends oriented in different positions: up, down, to the left, to the right, and at various angles to the horizontal. Then water the soil appropriately and shield the seeds from light by taping the cardboard over the front of the container. Place the planter in an area that provides a suitably warm temperature and allow it to remain undisturbed for 4-5 days. Remove the light shield and view the root growth that has developed. Observe the direction in which the roots are growing, and determine what adjustments, if any, are being made by the developing plants to achieve this growth pattern. On the basis of the data collected, draw a conclusion concerning the direction in which plant roots grow when seeds are planted in a garden, flower pot, or other planter.

EXPERIMENTS THAT ALLOW
STUDENTS TO TEST
THE VALIDITY OF HYPOTHESES

After they have carefully considered all the facts surrounding a situation, students should be encouraged to make an educated guess to explain what has been observed. This proposed answer to a question or problem constitutes a *hypothesis*, which is one of the most creative parts of science. Of course, not all guesses, no matter how educated, are necessarily correct. Each must be tested by a specifically designed experiment, and throughout the testing procedure the experimenter must keep an open mind. He must be ready and willing to give up his original belief if the experiment provides answers that are not in agreement with his prediction.

While performing a wide range of high interest level experiments which focus attention on the testing of hypotheses, students can develop important skills and gain experience in the methods by which the validity of the scientific hypotheses can be tested.

EXPERIMENT: COMPARING THE WATER VOLUME OF SNOW AND RAIN

Problem: How much water results from melting a tubeful of snow?

Hypothesis: Based on observations made in the past, write a tentative answer to the problem and record it in a notebook.

Procedure: Collect some snow, on a day when it is available, and pack it into a tube to a height of 30 cm. Mark the level of the snow in the tube, using a marking pen. Place the tube in a warm location and allow the snow to melt. When all of the snow has melted, measure and mark the water level in the tube. Compare the two markings on the tube and determine how much water results from snow which has melted. Relate this to the comparable amount of water resulting from a heavy snow storm.

EXPERIMENT: SEPARATING SOLUBLE AND INSOLUBLE SUBSTANCES

Problem: What happens to the soluble and insoluble substances in a liquid when the material is passed through a filter?

Hypothesis: Recall all information learned about soluble and insoluble substances and about filters. In your notebook write what you think the answer to the problem will be.

Procedure: Stir table salt into 50 ml. of water in a glass until no more salt will dissolve. Add 5 ml. of powdered chalk to the solution, stirring as before, and set the glass aside for a few moments.

Hang a partially unbent paper clip over the top of a clean glass jar. Line a funnel with folded filter paper and then support the funnel atop the collecting jar with paper clip positioned to prevent a build-up of pressure that would interfere with the filtering operation. Stir the liquid once more and pour it quickly into the filter paper. When all of the liquid has passed through, observe the two fractions:

1. Unfold the filter paper and spread it on a flat surface to dry and identify the substance held back by the filter.
2. Observe the clear filtrate in the collecting jar and determine what it is by touching the index finger first to the liquid and then to the tongue.

EXPERIMENT: INVESTIGATING SOILLESS GARDENING

Problem: Do plants need soil to grow?

Hypothesis: Make an "educated guess" in answer to the problem. Write this answer in your notebook, giving reasons to support your "guess."

Procedure: Place 1.5 g. of non-nutrient agar in 100 ml. of cold water and dissolve by heating to the boiling point. Allow to boil for 1 minute and cool slightly. Pour the liquid to a depth of 1 cm. into several petri dishes and allow to remain undisturbed at room temperature for 1 hour. When the agar has cooled and solidified, place three viable pumpkin, squash, radish, or bean seeds on the agar surface of each dish. Pour 3 ml. of water over each group of seeds. Invert a drinking glass or a glass jar over each petri dish, as shown in Figure 6-2. Then place the "planters" in a moderately lighted area that provides a fairly constant 20° C. temperature and avoids direct sunlight.

Examine the growth chambers daily, adding 3 ml. of water every second day to replenish the

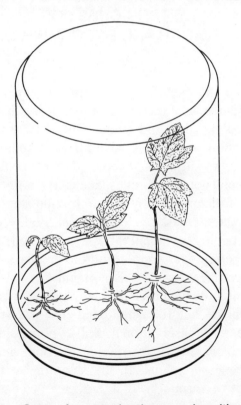

Figure 6-2. Setup for germinating seeds without soil.

water that has been used. Examine the seeds each day, placing the dishes for the first few days on a black background and using a hand lens to detect the appearance of delicate root hairs. Keep a record of the progress being made as the roots become more developed and stems and leaves also make an appearance. If seeds of more than one species have been planted, compare their growth and appearance and determine if this method of growing plants could be adapted for man to use in a practical manner.

EXPERIMENTS THAT REQUIRE EFFECTIVE TECHNIQUES FOR OBSERVATION AND RECORDING OF DATA

The manner in which students make observations is a key factor in the success of any experiment they perform. They must, of course, make careful observations that are directed toward a goal that they understand. But, to be of any real value, the observations made must also relate to something that the students want to know, and encouragement should be given for making special note of any unusual observations that suggest an extension of the experiment in a follow-up study. The experiments, of course, must be closely supervised, especially when matters pertaining to student safety are involved, and advantage must be taken of every opportunity to emphasize that "a successful experiment is a *safe* experiment."

Experiments which emphasize the recording of data and information are helpful when used to assist students in the development of observational skills. For example, designs should be included which provide for both quantitative and qualitative measurements. In the recording of the data in its most effective form—be it a drawing, a chart, or a word description—the observations become an organized part of the experimental study.

EXPERIMENT: DETERMINING THE AMOUNT OF WATER IN SOIL

Problem: How much water is found in a soil sample?

Procedure: Locate a garden or woodland area for obtaining a suitable soil sample for testing. Then fill a small container with material that can be collected from within 5 cm. of the surface and that contains no rocks, plant material, or debris.

Using a pan balance, weigh a 20-cm aluminum pie plate to the nearest gram and record its weight. Then weigh out 50 g. of the soil sample and place it in the pie plate, spreading it evenly. Place the pie plate containing the soil sample in a portable oven in the classroom and heat it for 4 hours at a temperature of 110° C. If no oven is available in the classroom, obtain permission to use one in the school lunchroom or cooking room, or arrange to transport this segment of the experiment home where a kitchen oven can be used while a parent supervises the activity. At the end of the heating/drying treatment, while wearing protective insulated safety mitts and being closely supervised by an adult, remove the pie plate from the oven, allow it to cool, and weigh again. Compare the weight of the pie plate and soil before and after the drying treatment and determine the weight of the water that evaporated during the heating process. Next subtract the weight of the pie plate to determine the dry weight of the soil alone and finally, calculate the percent of water in the soil sample.

EXPERIMENT: DETERMINING THE ABSORPTIVE
PROPERTIES OF A SPONGE

Problem: How much water can a sponge hold?

Procedure: Cut a large cellulose sponge (15 cm. by 10 cm. by
4.5 cm.) in half so that its length is cut to 7.5 cm.
Place the 7.5-cm. sponge in an aluminum pie
plate and weigh the sponge and plate together on a
pan balance. Transfer the sponge to a bucket of
water and allow it to soak for 3 minutes. Then
remove the sponge, allowing the excess water to
drip back into the bucket, but do not press or
squeeze the sponge. Place the wet sponge back
into the aluminum plate and weigh again. Record
the weight of the wet sponge and determine the
increase in weight due to water that was absorbed.

Examine the sponge to determine how it is
constructed to hold water.

EXPERIMENT: INVESTIGATING THE EVAPORATION
OF WATER BY PLANT LEAVES

Problem: How much water is lost through leaves of a plant?

Procedure: Fill a large pan with water and cut a leafy stem
from a sturdy house plant (such as a geranium) of
a suitable size to fit tightly into a piece of rubber
tubing. Apply vaseline around the cut end of the
stem, 1 cm. back from the cut surface, and similarly around the upper end of a 1-ml. pipette or
length of glass tubing.
Insert the greased end of the pipette into a 40-cm.
length of rubber tubing of appropriate diameter.
Then, place the stem end of the leafy branch
under water and, under supervision of the
teacher, use a single-edged razor blade to carefully cut off a thin slice. Discard the thin slice but

allow the branch to remain in water. Fill both the rubber tubing and pipette with water, taking care to avoid trapping any air bubbles.

While holding the tubing under water, insert the end of the branch into the tubing, allowing the vaseline to act as a seal. Remove the plant and tubing from the pan of water, holding the end of the glass higher than the plant. Tape the plant and tubing to a window, as shown in Figure 6-3, making certain that the glass tubing is in a vertical position. Using a glass marking pen, mark the water level in the pipette. If glass tubing is used,

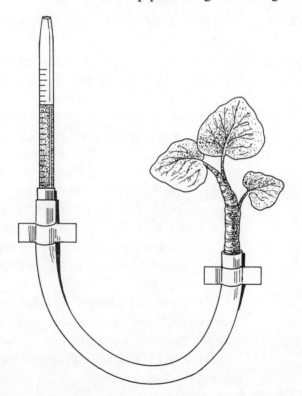

Figure 6-3. Setup for measuring water uptake by a leafy houseplant

place a small test tube or vial over the upper end of the tube to reduce the loss of water due to evaporation.

Allow the entire assembly to remain for 1-2 hours. Then observe the level of water in the pipette and measure how much water has been taken up by the leafy shoot in the allotted time. On the basis of observations made, write a conclusion about the uptake of water by a leafy plant.

EXPERIMENT: INVESTIGATING THE RESPIRATION OF YEAST CELLS

Problem: How does temperature affect the rate at which yeast cells respire?

Procedure: Dissolve 50 g. of sugar in 500 ml. of water. Then add one package of dry baker's yeast to the mixture, stirring gently to ensure an even distribution of all materials. Fill two large test tubes with the yeast-sugar mixture and invert them in separate glass jars containing a reserve supply of the mixture, making certain that none of the mixture escapes from the tubes in the process. Carefully place one of the assembled jars in a cool location in the room, and place the other in a warm location of constant temperature where there are no drafts. Allow the two assemblies to remain undisturbed for 24 hours.

The next day observe and measure the column of gas that has collected in each tube. Compare the two and determine how temperature affected the rate at which the yeast cells were respiring and producing CO_2 gas in the process. On the basis of the results of the experiment, suggest reasons why bread dough is traditionally placed in a warm location to "rise."

EXPERIMENT: DETERMINING THE VITAMIN C CONTENT IN ORANGE JUICE

Problem: Is there more vitamin C in fresh or canned orange juice?

Procedure: Pour the juice squeezed from a fresh orange into a clean glass. Into a second glass of the same size, pour an equal amount of real orange juice that has been canned or juice concentrate that has been diluted according to the package directions. Weaken the strength of the juice in each glass by adding water equal to the amount of juice.

        Next dissolve 1 g. of indophenol powder in 1 l. of water to prepare a 0.1 percent solution of indophenol, a chemical whose blue color fades when acted upon by ascorbic acid (vitamin C). Using a clean medicine dropper, place ten drops of indophenol solution in each of two clean test tubes. Using another clean dropper of the same size, add diluted fresh orange juice, drop by drop, to the indophenol in one of the tubes, shaking the test tube after the addition of each drop until the blue color disappears. Count and record the number of drops of fresh orange juice that were used. Then, using another clean dropper, add the diluted canned juice to the second prepared tube, again counting the number of drops needed to bleach out the color of the dye. Based on the data collected, determine if fresh or canned orange juice contains the greater amount of vitamin C.

EXPERIMENTS THAT INVOLVE KEEPING A *CONTROL* FOR COMPARISON

Students enjoy performing experiments which allow them to investigate how conditions may affect the outcome of an event. In these experiments every effort must be made to limit the testing to one factor at a time so that the outcome can be safely attributed to the condition that was altered and not to the general conditions that prevail.

Controlled experiments can be designed with a built-in control feature which serves as a check on the validity of the whole experiment. Setting up and running two experiments— the *experimental* and the *control*—in parallel provides a simple and convenient design: all factors except one are made identical in both setups, while only the variable factor is made different in the two. When the outcomes of the experimental and control situations are compared, any significant differences noted will provide information necessary for determining the effect of the condition tested on the outcome.

**EXPERIMENT: INVESTIGATING THE INFLUENCE OF
HEAT ON THE RATE OF EVAPORATION**

Problem: How does raising the temperature affect the rate of evaporation?

Procedure: Tie a string around the center of a meter stick so that the stick is balanced when supported by the string. Attach the other end of the string to an overhead support, keeping the stick balanced while being held in a horizontal position.

Next prepare two identical rectangular sponges to be hung from opposite sides of the meter stick: using a large darning needle and string, thread a piece of string through one corner of a sponge and tie the string so that the loop that is formed will slip over the end of the meter stick. Wet the sponges by dipping them into a bucket of water so that they are equally wet, but not dripping, and hang the wet sponges on opposite sides of the meter stick, sliding the string loops back and forth until the positions are located at which the system remains in balance. Then, under the close supervision of the teacher, and while practicing all proper safety precautions:

1. Place an electric hot plate directly below one of the sponges so that the distance between the sponge and hot plate is about 15 cm.
2. Adjust the hot plate temperature setting to produce medium high heat.
3. Observe what happens to the sponges that were balanced at the same level before the heating of the air around them.

On the basis of the observation, form a conclusion concerning how warming the surrounding air affects the rate of evaporation.

EXPERIMENT: DETERMINING THE EFFECT OF SALT ON THE RATE OF EVAPORATION

Problem: Does the addition of salt change the rate at which tap water evaporates?

Procedure: Pour 100 ml. of tap water into a heat-proof glass container. Into an identically-shaped container pour 100 ml. of a 5 percent salt solution. Leave the containers uncovered and, with the teacher present to supervise that segment of the activity involving the use of a heating device, place them side by side on an electric hot plate with the heat setting placed at "LOW." Evaporate the water from the two containers, noting the time that is required for the evaporation of the fresh water and of the salt water. Suggest reasons why this difference in rate of evaporation may be attributed to the salt rather than to another factor such as light or temperature, and apply this information to the evaporation of water from a fresh water lake and from an ocean.

EXPERIMENT: DETERMINING THE EFFECT OF PLANT GROWTH SUBSTANCES ON GERMINATING SEEDS

Problem: How does gibberellin affect the germination of pea seeds?

Procedure: Prepare two petri dishes in the following manner: line each dish with three or four circles of absorbent paper toweling and distribute five viable pea seeds over the surface. To one dish, designated the *experimental* dish, add 20 ml. of the plant hormone gibberellin. To the other, the *control*, add 20 ml. of plain water. Cover both dishes and place them in a warm location of subdued light. After 4-5 days, measure the lengths of the roots of every seed in each group. Record the data and calculate the average growth of the seeds for the "treated" and for the "control" groups. Note any differences observed between the seedlings developed from seeds supplied with growth hormones and from those given water only and suggest reasons for the differences in appearance and in growth.

EXPERIMENT: INVESTIGATING CORN THAT "POPS"

Problem: What makes popping corn pop?

Procedure: Obtain about forty kernels of popping corn and divide the sample equally to form two groups:
    1. The *experimental* group: pierce the seed coat of each kernel with a needle or a pin to allow the small amount of water contained within each kernel to escape.
    2. The *control* group: do not pierce the seed coats.

      Place each group of kernels in a separate flask containing a small amount of cooking oil.

Insert a loose-fitting stopper into the neck of each flask. Then, under close supervision of the teacher, employ proper safety measures while gently heating both flasks over a heat source and occasionally shaking the flasks and their contents until some popcorn is produced. Compare the results of the samples in which kernels had been pierced with those that had not. On the basis of the experiment, determine the importance of the small amount of water normally in a corn kernel with its capacity for popping. Trace the chain of events in which heating causes the formation of steam and a sudden expansion that, in turn, causes the kernel to explode and the white material to fluff up.

EXPERIMENTS THAT ARE OPEN-ENDED

Participating in open-ended experiments that encourage discovery gives students a feeling of how scientists work while engaging in a search for new information. Each conclusion drawn from data collected is not necessarily the bottom line; rather, conclusions drawn from one experiment may serve as the basis for formulating new hypotheses which are then similarly tested.

There are many opportunities for student input in the planning, execution, and follow-up of the open-ended experiment. With encouragement to observe thoughtfully and question every aspect of an experiment, students gradually develop an attitude toward science that ''experiments lead to other experiments, and learning leads to more learning.''

EXPERIMENT: INVESTIGATING THE WARMING
OF THE EARTH BY RADIANT ENERGY

Problem: Are sand and water warmed equally by the sun?

Procedure: Obtain two identically-shaped aluminum pie pans about 20 cm. in diameter. In one pan place 500 g. of sand; in the other, place 500 ml. (weight, 500 g.) of water. Then place a thermometer in each pan so that the thermometer bulbs are submerged to the same depth. Using two 100-watt electric light bulbs, suspend one bulb above each pan at a height of 15 cm. from the top of the pan. Record the temperature of the sand and of the water in their respective pans. Then turn on the lamps and record the temperature readings taken at 5-minute intervals over a 30-minute time period. Analyze the data collected. On the basis of the comparative study, draw a conclusion relating to the warming of sand and water at the beach on a sunny day.

EXPERIMENT: INVESTIGATING PRESSURE AND REGELATION

Problem: Does the amount of pressure applied affect the rate of regelation?

Procedure: Prepare two identically-shaped ice blocks, obtained from a refrigerator freezing tray, for regelation under different amounts of pressure.

1. Suspend a metal wire over one ice block and attach a 500-g. weight to each end of the wire.
2. Suspend a metal wire over the second ice block and attach a 1000-g. weight to each end of the wire.

Support both blocks on a narrow ledge so that the weights can move downward as the wires cut through the ice, as shown in Figure 6-4. Record the starting time and observe the two ice blocks. Determine the time required for each to

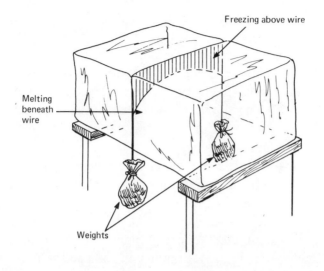

Figure 6-4. Setup for study of relationship between pressure and rate of regelation

melt under pressure and then refreeze. On the basis of the observations, draw a conclusion about the effect of pressure on the rate of regelation.

EXPERIMENT: INVESTIGATING INTERNAL AND EXTERNAL BODY TEMPERATURE

Problem: Does the internal body temperature change when the external temperature is lowered?

Procedure: Fill a large basin with cold water whose temperature is considerably lower than that of the classroom. Using a thermometer submerged in the water, monitor the temperature and maintain it within the range of 12-15° C. by adding ice cubes as needed.

Select a classmate to be the experimental subject in the experiment. Using an oral thermometer, take his body temperature and record the temperature in degrees Celsius. Then ask him to place his lower arm, up to the elbow, in the cold water in the basin. Have him keep his hand and forearm submerged while he sits quietly for 5 minutes with the oral thermometer in his mouth. During this time, continue to maintain the temperature of the water in the basin by adding ice when needed.

After 5 minutes have elapsed, remove his hand and forearm from the water, quickly damp-dry an area on his arm, and use a thermometer to take the temperature of his skin at this point. Again take his oral temperature and record both temperatures. Compare the oral and skin temperatures and determine if lowering the external temperature caused a change in the internal body temperature. Suggest applications of this observation to the internal body temperature when you go outside on a cold day in February.

Performing experiments helps to take some of the mystery out of science by providing opportunities to participate in discovery. The experiment provides opportunities for student input in the planning and preparation in addition to giving breadth to the range of activities for elementary school students by providing them with opportunities to make their own observations, to formulate hypotheses, and to seek explanations independent of the teacher. Experiments are accompanied by some very valuable outcomes: they involve high level thinking and problem solving on the part of the students, who derive much personal satisfaction from the experience.

7

Activities for Performing Demonstrations by Students

Students tend to develop greater enthusiasm for learning when they become involved individually in occasional change-of-pace activities. For example, opportunities to show others something they have discovered or learned helps to stimulate and reinforce a student's own learning while also contributing to the learning of others. Employing the technique of *student-demonstrations* is compatible with the educational approach that encourages students to help each other and to learn from one another in an atmosphere of sharing—and with the happy result that all students learn more!

Student demonstrations evolve naturally in the tradition of SHOW AND TELL activities, made popular in the primary grades. When adapted for use specifically for science on the elementary level, the demonstrations need to be designed to emphasize the ''show'' aspect of the presentations, to focus on topics and/or techniques that are directly related to current studies, and to be employed in a flexible manner to accommodate individual ability levels and areas of special interest.

There are many advantages that accrue from the inclusion of student-performed demonstrations in the program of science activities.

- They help the students to build self-confidence.
- They help in the development of special talents possessed by individual students.
- They serve to enrich and to extend the science program.

- They lend variety to the *science activities* for students.
- They provide opportunities for recognition of individual achievements and contributions.
- They may be used to stimulate interest in a topic that is being introduced, to develop further some aspect of a topic being studied currently, or to review a topic that has been studied previously.
- They may illustrate effectively some study topics for which there are no other hands-on components provided.

There is a need, however, to make a clear distinction between student demonstrations and those performed by the teacher as an integral part of the structured program of instruction. Student demonstrations should place no rigorous demands on students other than to encourage them in a supportive manner to become actively involved in the planning, preparation, and presentation of something scientific that they know and understand and can show to others. Actually, student demonstrations that have been found to be the most successful and to hold the attention of other students in the group are simple in design, fast moving, and of short duration. As is the case with all demonstrations, of course, an element of suspense can add to the excitement of student-performed demonstrations and should be included, if at all possible. But, above all, student demonstrations must be engaged in on a purely voluntary basis. They must provide enjoyable and rewarding experiences that enhance individual enthusiasm through active involvement and that promote personal growth and positive attitudes toward the learning of science.

DEMONSTRATIONS ILLUSTRATING SOME IMPORTANT GENERALIZATIONS IN SCIENCE

In elementary science, students are introduced to many generalizations relating to topics such as energy, matter, magnets, motion, gravity, and levers. To ensure that these be viewed as true generalizations rather than as mere associations with isolated cases of scientific "laws" and/or "principles," much reiteration is needed. A wide array of situations which illustrate generalizations as they apply to a class of objects, conditions, or events is needed, as is exposure to the many aspects of a given generalization that may alert students to the fact that in some cases generalizations in science need to have some qualifications.

Students can be encouraged to seek out appropriate topics and situations that can be demonstrated to others. The main thrust of a demonstration should be the *showing* of a generalization as it applies to a situation not previously known to other members of the group. The demonstrator is placed in the role of a classmate who has pursued an important aspect of science which he can now show, with understanding, to others; and those watching the demonstration can view the demonstration as a challenge to recognize and identify the generalization involved in a new setting or application. The sharing of information increases student understanding of scientific knowledge and contributes to the enjoyment and satisfaction of all students who perform demonstrations for each other. Performed under the direct supervision of the teacher, the demonstrations also allow for additional student practice in the employment of proper science skills and procedures and for a further reinforcement of the importance of strict adherence to the highest standards for student safety in science.

DEMONSTRATION: PRODUCING SOUNDS OF VARYING PITCH

Thoroughly clean several identical bottles of the tall narrow variety used for the 300-350 ml. size of fruit juice or soft drinks such as Coca Cola or a popular brand of soda pop. Pour a different amount of tap water into each bottle to produce a graduated series, such as: empty, ⅛ full, ¼ full, ½ full, ¾ full, and ⅞ full. Holding the empty bottle vertically to your lips, blow across the top of the bottle so that the pitch of the sound produced can be heard clearly. Taking each bottle in its turn—from the smallest to the largest amount of water it contains—repeat the procedure, and relate the pitch of the sound produced in each case to the corresponding length of the column of air vibrating above the water. If possible, by using a pitch pipe and adjusting the amount of water in each bottle, calibrate each bottle in the series to produce a different note of the musical scale. Then enlist the aid of a few classmates and orchestrate your own rendition of a popular tune or school song to be played on the bottles.

DEMONSTRATION: THE EFFECT OF HEAT
ON AIR PRESSURE

Practicing extreme caution while the teacher supervises, drop a piece of burning paper into a milk bottle. Watch carefully and at the instant the flame goes out, place the palm of your hand over the mouth of the bottle. Hold your hand in this position for a full minute. Then raise your hand and show what happens.

DEMONSTRATION: CREATING AIR CURRENTS
THAT CAN BE OBSERVED

Obtain a large plastic garment bag of the type used by dry cleaners, and make it airtight at the top by sealing the hanger opening with masking tape. Then, at the top center, attach a spring-type clothespin to be used for easy handling.

Next, make a wire ring to attach to the bottom edge of the bag: use thin wire to make a circle with two diameters that touch at their point of crossing at the center and wedge an absorbent cotton ball at this center point. Fold the bottom edge of the garment bag around the wire ring and fasten it with tape so that the bag is held open in a wide circle at its lower edge. Suspend the bag by the clothespin hanger until needed.

Protect the area to be used for the demonstration: place

aluminum foil on the floor, covering an area somewhat larger than that of the lower edge of the bag. Then, under the close supervision of the teacher, continue with the demonstration. Holding the bag by its clothespin hanger, suspend it so that its open end is positioned several centimeters above the protected floor area. Finally, wet the cotton ball with alcohol, ignite the alcohol, and observe closely. Note particularly what happens to the air in the bag and to the bag* itself. Describe the currents of air and tell what set them into motion.

DEMONSTRATION: THE FORCE OF INERTIA

Stack several books on a desk or tabletop. With both hands, grasp the book at the bottom of the stack and grip it securely. Then give it a quick jerk as you remove it from its position at the bottom of the stack. Note what happens to the books that were piled on top of the one that was removed. Inertia causes them to remain relatively undisturbed in a stack on the table top.

DEMONSTRATION: CENTRIFUGAL FORCE

Obtain a small bucket and fill it nearly full with water. Hold the handle in one hand. Then, with the teacher supervising the demonstration, swing the bucket around rapidly in a full circle while it is being held at arm's length. Observe that the water does not spill out of the bucket. This is due to centrifugal force.

DEMONSTRATION: THE EFFECTS OF LIGHT
ON A RADIOMETER

Place a radiometer on a table and view it in conditions of reduced light. Notice the construction of the instrument (shown

---

*The plastic bag is not flammable. If placed directly in a flame, however, it might melt.

Figure 7-1.   A radiometer for measuring radiant energy

in Figure 7-1) which consists of vanes or paddles mounted on a
needle in a partial vacuum. Observe that one surface of each
vane is bright and shiny; the other is dull and black. Using a
flashlight, increase the amount of light falling on the radiometer
and observe what happens. Remove the light source and continue to observe. Note the changes in activity as the light source
is alternately applied and removed. Then place the radiometer
in bright sunlight, observe again, and associate the activity of
the instrument with the amount of light falling upon it.

DEMONSTRATION: THE RELATIVE DENSITIES
OF LIQUIDS AND SOLIDS

Obtain a tall wide-mouth glass jar and a collection of
liquids and solids of different densities. Handle all materials

with care and take precautions to employ proper procedures when working with chemicals. Pour a layer of mercury to a depth of several centimeters in the jar, and then float a flat iron washer on the surface of the mercury. Next, so as not to disturb the mercury layer, carefully introduce a layer of carbon tetrachloride, allowing it to run down the inside wall of the jar. When this layer is several centimeters deep, float a small piece of ebony wood on its surface. Similarly, add a layer of water and a cube of paraffin floating on its surface, and finally a layer of kerosene and a small cork floating on top. Examine the vertical column which positions liquids and solids in an alternating sequence. Note that each liquid floats upon another of greater density, and that each solid floats at the interface between a liquid of greater density and a liquid of lesser density than that of the solid object.

DEMONSTRATIONS INVOLVING
SCIENTIFIC PHENOMENA

The unusual nature of scientific phenomena imbues them with a built-in attraction that is timeless and that commands attention. An eclipse of the sun or the moon, for example, is a physically observable event whose occurrence is viewed as widely today as it was by the ancients—but with a very important difference: while they viewed the phenomenon with awe and superstition, we view it today with awe and understanding.

Learning to discover and understand how and why natural phenomena occur is one of the primary concerns of science. Also, the fact that many phenomena can be demonstrated makes them prime targets for study and investigation at all levels. Students can make models in miniature from easy-to-obtain materials and can simulate natural events simply and without elaborate equipment. Relying on simple equipment and a direct approach, they can avoid the risk that the phenomenon being demonstrated will be obscured, and by taking sufficient care to check out all elements of the demonstration in successful trial runs, they can avoid the embarrassment and disappointment of a no-show demonstration.

DEMONSTRATION: A WEATHER "FRONT"

Partially fill four or five plastic bags with sand. Twist and tie a knot in the top of each bag to prevent the sand from spilling out. Then refrigerate the bags for several hours. Fill a small plastic bowl with hot water and place it, uncovered, in the bottom of one end of a glass aquarium tank. Place the cold sandbags in the aquarium tank at the end opposite the bowl of hot water. Place a cover over the top of the aquarium tank and observe the pattern of clouds that forms. Also observe the moisture that collects on the sides of the tank. Trace the pathway of cold air as it moves from the area above the sandbags, under and into the warm moist air above the bowl of hot water. It demonstrates a *cold front* boundary along which the cold air moves toward a region of warmer air.

DEMONSTRATION: A SHIP "RIDING THE WAVES" IN A BOTTLE

Prepare an attention-getting demonstration using only a large flat-sided bottle, shellac thinner, colorless paint thinner, green vegetable food coloring, and a small wooden ship model of appropriate size for the bottle.

Select a bottle that can be tightly stoppered and placed on its side for viewing. Fill the bottle one-third full of shellac thinner and add one drop of green food coloring material. Next, add colorless, odorless paint thinner to completely fill the bottle, carefully insert a small wooden ship model to which weights have been attached, tightly cap the bottle, and place it on its side on a desk or table for testing. Make adjustments as needed in the weight of the ship until it just floats at the interface between the two liquids.

When adjusted, lift the stoppered bottle gently at one end, and set it down again. Observe the wave that appears at one end of the green liquid as the bottle is tilted. Continue to observe as the wave moves slowly to the other end of the bottle, reverses its direction, and moves slowly back again to the end that had originally been uplifted. Reverse the procedure, lifting the opposite end of the bottle, and observe again. Encourage individual classmates to repeat the procedure again and again while they make observations of a simulation of a ship in turbulent waters.

DEMONSTRATION: LEVITATION

Obtain two small bar magnets of the same size and show that two unlike magnetic poles (N and S) are attracted to each other, while two like poles (N and N or S and S) repel each other. Place one of the magnets on the surface of a flat block of styrofoam and, using six toothpicks, build a fence around the magnet by sticking toothpicks into the styrofoam close to the four sides of the magnet. Carefully hold the second magnet between the toothpicks, keeping the S pole of the top magnet over the S pole of the magnet on the bottom. Gently lower the magnet ever so slightly, and then release it. Allow all classmates to observe that the upper magnet does not fall beyond a certain point; rather, due to an interaction of the magnetic fields of force, it floats above the lower one. By showing how an object can be suspended in the air without any material support, you have given a demonstration of *levitation*.

DEMONSTRATION: STATIC ELECTRICITY

I. Spread out a piece of newspaper and press it smoothly against a wall area in a room in which the air is very dry. Stroke the entire surface of the newspaper many times with the long side of a pencil. Next, pull up one corner of the paper and then release it. Observe what happens and describe both what you see and what you hear.

II. Obtain an aluminum baking pan, a glass plate to cover it, and some thin tissue paper from which to cut small doll figures that are somewhat shorter than the depth of the pan. Cut the figures in the shape of dancers or boxers, or in the form of familiar animals such as frogs or birds. Then put the paper figures in the bottom of the pan and place the glass cover over the top. Rub the top surface of the glass with a piece of fur or soft leather, watch the doll figures, and describe their activity.

III. Inflate a balloon and tie a knot in its neck to prevent the air from escaping. Rub the balloon on your sleeve and then take it close to a wall or ceiling of the room. If it is a dry day it may remain on the wall or ceiling for quite a long time. Recapture your balloon and place it near a classmate's balloon that has been rubbed briskly also. Note the repulsion that is demonstrated by the objects having the same electrical charges.

DEMONSTRATION: AN EARTHQUAKE

Place a long plastic tube into the neck of a strong balloon and make the connection airtight so that the balloon can be blown up later by using the tubing as an airline. Place the balloon in a protective plastic bag and lay the plastic-covered balloon in the bottom of a glass-walled aquarium tank, with the airline extending to the top of the tank and beyond. Cover the plastic bag with a layer of damp sand. On top of this spread a 2-mm. thick layer of dry sand. Then, alternately add layers of damp sand and dry sand until about eight layers, representing rock layers in the earth, have been formed. Slowly and gently blow air into the plastic tubing so that the balloon becomes filled with air very gradually. Watch for cracks to develop in the sand layers and for "faults" to occur near the surface. As pressure builds up in the balloon, the sand layers can be seen to crack just as the rock layers do during an earthquake.

DEMONSTRATION: TRANSPIRATION OF WATER FROM PLANT LEAVES

Obtain a small potted house plant and water the soil well. Place the pot in a plastic bag, drawing the plastic up to cover the soil and the lower part of the stem. Using a twistem-tie, make a tight fit around the plant stem so that no water can be lost by evaporation from the soil. Then invert a clean glass jar over the entire plant and allow the entire assembly to remain undisturbed for a few hours. Observe what has happened; note that droplets of moisture, condensed from water vapor released by the plant leaves, have formed on the inside of the jar.

DEMONSTRATIONS IN WHICH ALL STUDENTS PARTICIPATE

Demonstrations that place all students in the role of active participants involve them personally and individually as each student actually performs the demonstrations at the direction of a student "leader" who instructs his classmates in the proper procedures. The values are twofold: (1) students learn more effectively when they are personally and individually involved, and (2) students who may be hesitant about performing a demonstration *to* others may build self-cofidence by performing a demonstration *with* them.

Since these demonstration may involve large numbers of participants, they must revolve about topics of general interest and usage and must require only the simplest of materials with which to work. Techniques for employment in investigative work and topics relating to personal experiences for which there is no other hands-on component provided in the course of study can be demonstrated effectively and practiced by all students. Here the confidence factor builds significantly as students are encouraged to repeat the demonstrations to friends and family in an enjoyable way, thereby reinforcing their own understanding of something of scientific importance while sharing with others something they have learned.

DEMONSTRATION: LOCATION OF A BLIND SPOT

In well-separated positions on a white index card, draw a circle and a square such that the diameter of the circle and the sides of the square are of equal measure. (See Figure 7-2.) With your left hand cover your left eye, and with your right hand hold the card at arm's length in front of your face as you focus your right eye on the black circle. You will be able to see the square as well. Slowly move the card closer to your eye until you reach a point at which the square disappears from view. Your right eye is "blind" at this spot. Now move the card still closer until the square reappears.

Figure 7-2. Figure for demonstrating the blind spot

Repeat the procedure, and again locate the blind spot. This time, while holding the card steady in the "blind spot" position, remove your left hand from in front of your left eye and determine if both eyes have a blind spot at the same location. By inverting the card and covering the right eye, a left eye blind spot may be located in a similar manner.

DEMONSTRATION: MAKING A ST. PATRICK'S DAY CARNATION

Place the stem of a white carnation in a jar of water to which several drops of green food coloring have been added.

Allow it to remain undisturbed overnight and examine the appearance of the flower on the following day. Water transported from the jar upward in the stem to the flower enables the petals to maintain their fresh condition. The green coloring, also in the water, penetrates the flower petals, making them appear green.

DEMONSTRATION: HOW PHOTOGRAPHS ARE REPRODUCED IN NEWSPAPERS

Clip a black and white photograph from a newspaper and observe that many shades of both dark and light areas are present. Select three areas representing different intensities of gray in the photograph and mark off a 1-sq. cm. block in each. Then, using a magnifying lens, make a close examination of each of the blocks and determine how various shadings in a picture are achieved in newspapers, magazines, or on a television screen.

DEMONSTRATION: DETERMINATION OF EYE DOMINANCE

Roll a piece of paper lengthwise to make a funnel that is about 3 cm. in diameter at its far end. Use both hands to hold the funnel several centimeters in front of your face. With both eyes open, sight a distant object through the funnel. Then, alternately close one eye and then the other while you continue to view the same area. If the view shifts to the left or the right, the eye doing the viewing is not the dominant eye. The eye that sees the same object still in the same position as when viewed with both eyes open is the dominant eye.

DEMONSTRATION: EVAPORATION AS A COOLING PROCESS

I. Place several drops of alcohol on your hand or arm and allow them to dry. The coolness felt on the affected skin area demonstrates how the evaporation of perspiration cools your body.

II. To demonstrate the effects of heat and motion of molecules on the rate of evaporation, dip your hands in a basin of water to make them equally wet but not dripping. Hold your left hand quietly by your side while you swing your right arm around in a wide circle for about half a minute. Then examine your two hands and compare them to see which is drier and which feels cooler.

DEMONSTRATION: IMMOBILIZING INSECTS

Capture some insects and place them in a covered jar. Fill a small bowl with crushed ice and set the jar in the bowl of ice, allowing it to remain for about 10 minutes or until the insects become immobilized. This demonstrates the proper way to handle fast moving insects to be used for activities in which they are experimental subjects.

DEMONSTRATION: CARBON DIOXIDE
IN EXHALED BREATH

Using a soda straw, exhale your breath into a small amount of limewater until it turns from clear to a cloudy, milky white precipitate. This demonstrates that exhaled air contains carbon dioxide, which combines chemically with limewater to form a limestone-like product called calcium carbonate. When the water evaporates, the residue limestone can be seen accumulated in the bottom of the glass or jar.

DEMONSTRATION: "BULGING" OF THE EARTH
AT THE EQUATOR

Cut a piece of paper to form a strip about 30-40 cm. in length and about 2-3 cm. in width. Punch a hole in the middle of the strip so that a new eraser-topped pencil can be slipped through the hole. With the pencil in position, lift the ends of the paper strip up and bring them together so that a circle is formed. Using a thumbtack, attach the ends of the paper strip firmly to the eraser at the top of the pencil. With a brisk motion, roll the pencil back and forth while holding it between the palms of your hands. Observe what happens to the shape of the paper circle and relate it to centrifugal force. The bulging out at the middle gives the paper circle a somewhat flattened shape, similar to that of the earth at the equator.

DEMONSTRATION: HOW A JET ENGINE WORKS

Inflate a balloon and twist the neck tightly while holding it securely between your fingers. Then release the balloon. Observe what happens as the air escapes. This demonstrates the principle of action and reaction upon which the jet engine is based.

DEMONSTRATION: BERNOULLI'S PRINCIPLE

On a tabletop place two books with a space of about 10 cm. between them. Place a sheet of paper over the two books. Then blow your breath across the paper and observe what happens. The principle demonstrated is important in the field of aerodynamics.

DEMONSTRATIONS INVOLVING SUSPENSE AND EXCITEMENT

Suspense and speculation about the outcome are two important elements that lend excitement to a demonstration that is being performed. The very nature of a demonstration that elicits some serious thinking about its outcome holds students with rapt attention. If the demonstration is also prefaced by a thought-provoking question germane to the issue, or if the equipment displayed includes an unusual piece of apparatus not normally associated with science, interesting and thoughtful predictions concerning the outcome may be encouraged further. However, the actual viewing of a demonstration may be accompanied by some unexpected surprises! To safeguard all of the suspense and excitement surrounding demonstrations of this type, and to ensure that the value of this kind of learning situation will not be diminished by revealing information too soon, the demonstrator must be cautioned against divulging any pertinent information prior to the performance. The effectiveness of the demonstration depends primarily then on the demonstrator to *show* and on the watchers to *observe* and to *learn*.

DEMONSTRATION: BOILING WATER IN A PAPER CUP

Support a small unwaxed paper cup on a ring stand or inside a clay triangle mounted on a tripod. Fill the cup completely to the brim with warm water. Then, wearing protective goggles and using appropriate safety precautions for handling an open flame, use the flame of a bunsen burner or alcohol lamp to heat the paper cup directly over the flame, fanning the flame over the entire surface of the paper cup while the teacher supervises the activity.

Continue heating the cup in this manner until the water in the cup begins to boil. Verify the boiling point by taking a temperature reading of the water with a Celsius thermometer. Note that although the water is boiling, the paper cup is unchanged and has suffered no damage from the open flame. Ask classmates to volunteer reasons. If they are unable to do so, obtain two more identical cups. Fill one only partially with water and heat it in the manner described, noting that although the water here boils also, the top edges of the paper cup become charred; the other, with no water at all, burns when heated in the flame.

From the demonstration, classmates should learn and understand that a paper cup will burn in an open flame, but that if the cup contains water, the heat from the flame is quickly transferred to the water, taking heat away from the paper cup (which does not reach its kindling temperature) and transferring it to the water (which does reach its boiling point). Any paper unable to transfer the heat from the flame in this manner will, of course, burn.

DEMONSTRATION: LOSS AND RESTORATION OF COLOR IN A DYE SOLUTION

Under supervision of the teacher, practice all safety measures for safe handling of chemicals and dissolve 10 g. of sodium hydroxide (NaOH) in about 0.5 1. of distilled water. To this solution add 10 g. of dextrose, allowing it too to dissolve. Transfer the resulting solution to a 2-1. Erlenmeyer flask. Then add five drops of 5 percent methylene blue dye solution. Stopper the flask and observe as the blue color fades within a few minutes. Shake the flask vigorously and observe closely as the blue color reappears. Allow the material to settle and fade again; then shake once more to restore the blue color.

It should be noted that, in addition to the obvious change-in-color associated with the shaking and/or settling, the solution is brought into contact with the large air mass in the space above the level of the liquid in the flask during the shaking process. It is this combination with oxygen in the air that causes the colorless compound to regain its original color, i.e., the blue of methylene blue dye.

DEMONSTRATION: SPONTANEOUS COMBUSTION

Before beginning this activity, prepare a working area in a demonstration hood or on a table with a well-protected surface and a transparent safety shield. Also provide safety goggles for yourself and for the personal use of all viewers.

Place a tripod in the center of the working area, and on its upper surface place a 12.5-cm. square wire mesh screen and a 15-cm. circle of filter paper. While the teacher supervises the activity, place approximately 4 g. of potassium permanganate crystals in the center of the paper and, using a medicine dropper, add four or five drops of glycerine to the top of the pile of crystals. Place a second circle of 15-cm. filter paper lightly over the chemicals and, wearing safety goggles and standing at a safe distance, wait one suspenseful minute.

Heat generated during the chemical reaction causes a temperature rise. When the temperature reaches the kindling point of the paper, combustion occurs and the paper is observed to burst spontaneously into flame.

It is important to point out the demonstrated potential dangers to property and individual well-being and the necessity for employing appropriate safety measures here and in all science activities involving chemicals and potentially hazardous conditions.

DEMONSTRATION: ARCHIMEDES' PRINCIPLE

Use two consecutive mixing bowls of a set that is made of a transparent material and that can be nested together. First place the smaller bowl on the surface of the water in a large aquarium and allow everyone to observe that the bowl does indeed float. Then transfer this bowl to the one which is just slightly larger in size and into which 250 ml. of water has been poured. Note that the smaller bowl again floats—this time in only 250 ml. of water. Encourage classmates to observe that the bowl floats with a small as well as a large amount of water beneath it, and that when the contour of the container is the same as the floating object, it reduces further the amount of water needed to float the bowl. Encourage them also to consider how much water might be needed to float a battleship, suggesting by way of a clue, the principle upon which floating a ship in a "lock" is based. Finally, relate the demonstration in a general way to Archimedes' principle involving the displacement of water.

DEMONSTRATION: PING PONG BALL IN A FUNNEL

Obtain a funnel whose neck is too small for a Ping Pong ball to fit through and, holding the funnel in an upright position, place a Ping Pong ball in it as shown in Figure 7-3. Raise the funnel so you can blow through it. Then blow as hard as you can and try to blow the ball out.

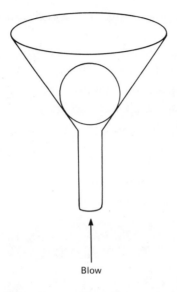

Blow

Figure 7-3. Setup for trying to blow Pong Pong ball out of a funnel

Next, invert the funnel, holding the ball in place with the palm of your hand. Take a deep breath, start blowing into the stem of the funnel, and remove your hand from the base as you continue to blow. Observe what happens to the ball.

To understand why the Ping Pong ball behaves as it does, trace the pathway of air being blown through the funnel and around the ball, and relate your observations to an important principle involving air pressure: moving air reduces the pressure on the surface over which it moves.

DEMONSTRATION: DANCING MOTHBALLS

Set a tall glass jar of about 1-l. capacity on a table top within clear view of all watchers. Pour water into the jar until it reaches approximately the half-full level. Then add a few drops of food coloring, 250 ml. of white household vinegar, six mothballs, and 3 g. of sodium bicarbonate. Observe closely as the mothballs begin to rise, reach the surface, and then sink to the bottom again, only to repeat the entire process many times over.

This is a real attention-getter. Encourage classmates to speculate, rather than ask why the mothballs rise and fall. See how many observe the accumulation of tiny gas bubbles on the surface of the mothballs just before they begin to rise, and their absence as the balls fall, and if they relate this to a change in density of the mothballs. See also if they can identify the gas as a product of the chemical reaction between the vinegar and the sodium bicarbonate that will continue for 1-2 hours or until the chemical components have created a stable condition.

DEMONSTRATION: FITTING PAPER CLIPS INTO A GLASS ALREADY FILLED WITH WATER

After placing a drinking glass on a level tabletop, fill it with tap water until it can hold no more. Then, carefully place paper clips, one at a time, into the water: hold each paper clip near one end, lower it with the other end partially beneath the surface of the water, and without splashing or causing an overflow release it, allowing it to drop to the bottom.

Keep a record of the number of paper clips that can be added in this manner. After each paper clip drops to the bottom of the glass, observe the appearance of the water's surface and note that each addition brings about a greater enlargement of the water's "bulge" over the rim. When the water eventually begins to spill over, stop adding paper clips and observe the pattern formed by the paper clips deposited in the bottom of the glass. Then ask classmates to suggest reasons why a glass full of water can still hold X number of paper clips.

When students show others something about which they have some knowledge, they gain self-confidence and are encouraged to learn more. By engaging in demonstration-type activities in which all students participate cooperatively, the spirit of sharing and learning from one another becomes contagious. As a result, the learning process is intensified.

8

Activities for Investigating and Employing Practical Applications of Science

One of the primary attractions associated with the more popular science activities is concerned with their recognized usefulness to man and the acknowledged relevance they have to conditions as we view them today. Happily, the elementary science curriculum abounds with opportunities for students to attach importance to what they have learned by applying scientific knowledge and methods to real problems and situations.

Science has an effect on everything. Engaging in activities that would investigate its applications to such a vast and wide array of topics requires some background information as well as familiarity and experience with scientific skills, techniques, and procedures on many fronts. By April most students have had this exposure (commensurate with their grade and ability levels), have developed (to some degree) an ability to work independently, and have had their science-consciousness elevated (by previous activities) sufficiently to consider the uses to which man puts the scientific information that he has discovered and learned. It is this usefulness of *science* in *real* situations with which the students can relate that is responsible for the ground swell of enthusiasm for this type of activity.

A program of activities for elementary students engaging in the ''practical'' aspects of science has two main thrusts:

1. Students must understand and attach meaning to the principles, techniques, or other elements of science that are involved in the activities.

2. Students must be able to relate and employ this understanding in useful and significant ways to a specific situation.

A program that addresses itself to these goals requires that each activity be very specific and carefully selected. The strategy is for students to investigate situations in which man's knowledge and understanding of science combines with his innovativeness to bring about a change that will improve a situation. There are also challenges for students to recognize some of the possible pitfalls and less-than-desirable consequences that may accompany these changes. Both long-range and immediate effects must be considered, as well as the consequences—with and without the practical application—to man.

Activities that focus on applications of science involve many previously employed approaches, including observing, demonstrating, experimenting, record-keeping, and analyzing and interpreting data collected. They are designed to enable students to view the impact that science has on practical matters such as labor-saving devices, food supply, plant and animal growth, and on man's well-being as he strives to improve his life while maintaining conditions of balance and harmony with his fellow creatures and with the environment. Their goal is to provide satisfying experiences that will lend further encouragement to students to learn and understand science and that will help them develop an appreciation of the contributions made by those who discover and learn, and then apply their scientific know-how to relevant and important situations.

One of the most important outcomes of activities that focus on practical applications is the development of positive attitudes toward science that prompt serious thought about other situations in which science might provide a better way of doing something. These thoughts, combined with the students' constantly growing independence and confidence with the *activities* approach, then act as a springboard from which topics they suggest can be pursued as independent study projects.

SCIENCE ACTIVITIES RELATING TO ASPECTS OF THE ENVIRONMENT

Currently, concern for the environment enjoys a top priority rating among scientists and the general public alike. The reasons are very practical in nature. The earth is constantly changing and these changes are continually affecting our lives —some directly, other indirectly; some beneficially, others harmfully.

Many activities can be designed to detect and evaluate environmental changes and to monitor and control those which might prove to have deleterious effects. Students engaging in these activities are usually surprised to learn that although some of the changes are brought about by man, others occur irrespective and independent of his activities. However, although he is not the sole instrument in bringing about change, man might very well be the only agent capable of exerting control over them. This places great responsibility upon man for being astute and applying scientific information both for use in detecting and evaluating changes and for planning and instituting corrective action.

ACTIVITY: INVESTIGATING ACID RAIN

During a rainstorm place a clean enamelware pan in an open area and collect some rainwater. Transfer the water collected to a clean glass jar. Then place a small sample of the rainwater in a dish or saucer and dip one end of a strip of blue litmus paper into the sample near its edge. Examine the color of the wet end of the litmus paper. Also observe the wetted end of a strip of red litmus paper, similarly applied to another edge of the sample. A red color will indicate the presence of an acid; a blue color will indicate a base.

All rainwater will be expected to show some acidity due to the chemical union of water with carbon dioxide in the atmosphere. Samples of rainwater collected from areas where smoke, smog, and other air pollutants such as gases containing oxides of sulfur and nitrogen are also present show a proportionately higher acid concentration. The more gases present to unite chemically with the water, the more acid the rain.

ACTIVITY: INVESTIGATING THE EFFECTS OF WAVES ON A SANDY BEACH

Place some beach sand in a deep tray and shape it with contours to form a sandy beach across one end of the tray. Slightly incline the tray by putting a block of wood under the beach end. While holding a wide sponge at the beach front, carefully pour water into the opposite end of the tray, filling it to about a half-full capacity. Then move the sponge rhythmically, back and forth, toward and away from the sandy beach to produce gentle waves. Notice the effect of the waves on the beach and suggest ways that beach erosion can be controlled.

ACTIVITY: INVESTIGATING THE EFFECTS OF WIND ON SOIL

Obtain a small bucketful each of clay, coarse sand, and gravel. Mix the materials well and place the mixture in a pile on the ground fairly close to the school building. While the teacher supervises the activity, stretch a long extension cord to an electric fan placed near the pile of clay, sand, and gravel. Keeping fingers away from the blades of the fan, turn on the fan so that the "wind" strikes the pile of soil. Allow the wind to blow for 5-10 minutes. Then examine what the effect of the wind has been. Determine which material has been most affected by the "windstorm," which has been affected the least, and what might be expected to happen if a stronger wind had been involved.

ACTIVITY: INVESTIGATING THE EFFECTS OF RAIN ON SOIL

Place a layer of garden soil in each of two rectangular flat boxes which provide for some drainage. Distribute some grass clippings or leaves evenly over the surface of the soil in one box. Allow the soil in the other box to remain bare.

Place both boxes in an open area during a rainstorm. After the rain has ended, remove the grass cover. Then examine and compare the soil surfaces in the two boxes. Transfer the boxes to a protected area and allow them to stand for 3 days. Examine the crust that is likely to form at the surface of the soil in both boxes, and determine what effect raindrops have had on the bare soil and what advantages are associated with soil surfaces that have had some cover.

ACTIVITY: FINDING DISSOLVED SOLIDS IN WATER

Under the supervision of the teacher, place a small pan about half-full of tap water on a hot plate. Position a clean dry glass square of appropriate size over the top of the pan. Then transfer about 10 ml. of water from a sample to be tested to the center of the glass plate, making a circular pool about 5 cm. in diameter. Turn on the hot plate and heat the water in the pan, allowing the water to boil vigorously until all of the water sample on the surface of the plate has evaporated.

After the plate has cooled, observe it closely for evidence of a residue. Then, in a similar manner, test clear-looking water samples taken from a lake, a reservoir, a well, a stream, and a river to detect the presence of solid impurities that may be dissolved in the water.

SCIENCE ACTIVITIES WHICH APPLY
TO PRODUCTS THAT ARE USEFUL TO MAN

Man's dependence upon science to provide him with products he needs and uses has been in evidence for centuries. Thousands of years ago the Chinese treated boils and infections with moldy tree bark and soil poultices. Some early American Indian tribes made adobe bricks from sun-dried earth and clay. Peoples the world over practiced methods of processing and preserving foods without really understanding why these methods were effective or without being able to take full advantage of their potential.

Scientific progress over the years has been accompanied by greater understanding of a larger fund of useful information that can be applied to a wider range of new and improved products for man—and the search for more continues in a never-ending pattern. There are many activities that provide students with opportunities to discover the role of science in supplying the products man needs and uses. But, unlike the early applications which ended when a method ''worked,'' today's emphasis is on understanding *why*, on expanding the applications to include more innovative measures, and in deriving intellectual growth and satisfaction in the process.

ACTIVITY: INVESTIGATING TIME-RELEASE CAPSULES

Open a CONTAC cold capsule over a shallow dish and pour the contents of the capsule into the dish. Using a magnifying lens observe the many tiny beads of different colors. Pour enough water into the dish to cover the tiny beads. Then note and record the time that it takes for some of the beads to burst, releasing their active ingredients and leaving their empty shells to float in the water. Similarly note and record the time for another group of beads to release their content. Continue the procedure until all beads have been ruptured and only empty shells can be detected in the water.

Each *bead* is a small unit of medication which is programmed to be released as soon as sufficient water has been absorbed by the coating to cause it to burst. Thinly-coated beads burst open first; more thickly-coated beads take longer, so that a time-release capsule is useful for supplying medication to a patient over a period of several hours without disturbing his rest and sleep.

ACTIVITY: MAKING WOOD STRONGER

In a well-ventilated area, while wearing safety goggles and working with the teacher, carefully measure and combine 4 g. of urea crystals, 25 ml. of formaldehyde, and 5 ml. of dilute hydrochloric acid in a clean glass jar. With a tongue depressor carefully stir the mixture and allow it to stand for a few minutes while you place two small flat pieces of wood on layers of paper toweling. Taking care to avoid spilling any of the material, pour some of the mixture in the jar over one surface of one of the wood pieces. Using the tongue depressor again, spread the mixture around so that it will soak in well. Similarly spread some of the mixture on the second piece of wood. Then place their wet surfaces together, sandwich-style, and tie a string around them so that they are held in tight contact with each other. Pour some of the mixture remaining in the jar through filter paper in a funnel. Then wedge some of the material that has collected on the filter paper into any spaces that appear around the outside edges between the two pieces of wood.

Place your "sandwich" between toweling and stack several heavy books on top of it. Allow it to remain undisturbed until the next day. At the end of a 24-hour time period, remove the books, toweling, and string, and examine the product you have made. Apply pressure and try to pull the two wood pieces apart. The product you have made is well-bonded, very strong, and resembles plywood.

ACTIVITY: MAKING CHEESE

Dissolve some powdered milk according to the directions supplied on the product label. Next place 250 ml. of this milk in a clean beaker and warm it gently on a hot plate to 32° C. While stirring, add 0.5 ml. of the enzyme *rennilase*. Then remove the beaker from the hot plate and allow it to stand undisturbed at room temperature.

After 15 minutes have elapsed, examine the content of the beaker and observe that the milk has coagulated and formed a solid called *curd*. Break up this curd and filter the resulting mash through clean cheesecloth to separate the whey from the curd. Discard the yellowish filtrate, the whey, and use the curd for cheesemaking: Add 1.5 g. of table salt to the curd and store the resulting *cottage cheese* in a refrigerator until it is to be eaten.

ACTIVITY: SEPARATING FRUIT JUICE FROM PULP

Place 50 g. of fresh or canned applesauce in a clean glass jar. Add 1 ml. of the enzyme *pectinase* and stir the mixture well until the enzyme is evenly distributed throughout the applesauce. Allow the mixture to stand for 5 minutes while you set up a clean graduated cylinder or measuring cup fitted with a funnel and filter paper. Then pour the applesauce mixture into the filtration system and measure the amount of filtrate that collects in the graduated cylinder or measuring cup. This liquid filtrate is apple juice which has been separated from the pulp remaining on the filter paper. To test the usefulness of pectinase in the process of separating apple juice from the fruit pulp, try to filter some applesauce to which pectinase has not been added.

ACTIVITY: MAKING HARD WATER SOFT

Obtain a 100 ml. sample of tap water which is known to be "hard" or untreated with water softeners. If necessary, make hard water by dissolving 1 g. of magnesium sulfate in 100 ml. of ordinary tap water.

Divide the sample into two parts, placing 50 ml. of hard water in each of two clean glass jars equipped with screw-cap covers. To one jar add one drop of Ivory liquid; to the other add

0.5 g. of sodium carbonate and one drop of the soap concentrate. Mark the jars for easy identification and screw on the jar tops tightly to prevent any leakage. Then shake the jars vigorously for 1 minute each and compare the quantity of suds produced in each. Set both jars on a table and allow them to remain undisturbed for at least 10 minutes. Make another examination to compare the lasting quality of the suds produced by one drop of soap in the treated and untreated samples of hard water.

The addition of sodium carbonate acts to soften hard water, allowing for more and lasting suds to be produced by the same amount of soap. This is important because hard water reduces the sudsing activity or requires that more soap be used for laundry or other household cleaning projects.

SCIENCE ACTIVITIES WHICH APPLY TO USEFUL INSTRUMENTS AND DEVICES

The fascination that many instruments and mechanisms hold for elementary students is very much in evidence when students are observed taking apart a timepiece, the mechanism of a music box, or any other device just to see how it works. Sometimes the intricacies of the mechanism are so great as to obscure any real understanding of its operation, but the fascination remains.

Activities that are simple in design and that involve mechanisms assembled from simple and common materials are best suited for illustrating how some scientific instruments and devices serve a useful purpose. Also, the more general the mechanism in use, the more effective the activity, because its employment in an everyday home or classroom situation reinforces learning and understanding with each usage.

ACTIVITY: MAKING A RAIN GAUGE

Support a clean plastic cylinder or any other flat-bottom

container with straight sides on a level board. Place the board with the attached container in an open space, keeping the entire assembly level at all times. Allow the container to collect rain as it falls during a rainstorm. Then, place one end of a millimeter tape or ruler against the bottom of the container. Holding the ruler in a vertical position, read the measurement of rainfall at the water mark. When the rain gauge is used to collect precipitation during a snowstorm, the snow must be allowed to melt before taking a measurement.

ACTIVITY: MAKING A HOMEMADE
FIRE EXTINGUISHER

Fill a wide-mouth bottle about two-thirds full of tap water into which 30 g. of baking soda have been dissolved. Next make a nozzle. Using all appropriate safety measures and with the guidance and supervision of the teacher, proceed with the steps that follow. Hold the ends of a short piece of glass tubing so that its middle is heated directly in the open flame of a bunsen burner. When the heated section becomes sufficiently softened, draw the two ends of the tube farther apart while causing the diameter of the middle section to become narrowed. Rest the tube on a heat-proof pad and allow it to cool. Then cut the tube across the middle, producing two pieces, and select one to serve as a nozzle for the activity. Insert the undrawn end of the tube into a one-hole rubber stopper that fits snugly into the neck of the bottle and allows the nozzle end to extend a few centimeters beyond the outer edge of the stopper. Also twist one end of a long wire around a small vial so that the vial can be suspended in an upright position when the wire is held vertically.

Observe closely the safety precautions taken as the teacher fills the vial with a solution of dilute hydrochloric acid. Note also the extreme care taken as she lowers the wire into the bottle until the vial is suspended about 1 cm. above the level of the soda solution. Then, while under close supervision of the teacher, complete the assemblage of the extinguisher and test its performance.

1. Insert the stopper tightly into the neck of the bottle and, using another piece of wire for the purpose, fasten the stopper securely to the top of the bottle.
2. Turn the extinguisher upside down over a sink.

When the acid pours from the vial into the soda solution, there is a chemical reaction in which carbon dioxide gas is produced. The pressure created by the gas forces a spray of the carbon dioxide mixed with water out through the nozzle. If directed onto some burning material, the water lowers the temperature of the burning fuel and the carbon dioxide forms a blanket which smothers the fire by keeping out the oxygen. Thus a fire may be extinguished.

ACTIVITY: MAKING A SOLAR OVEN

Carefully lay two long strips of heavy aluminum foil lengthwise to cover a 75 cm. by 200 cm. piece of sturdy wrapping paper. Glue the foil layer to the paper, making certain that both surfaces lie flat and that there are no wrinkles. Allow the glue to dry thoroughly. Then, holding the shiny surfaces toward the inside, roll the foil-lined paper into an inverted cone. Trim away all excess material at the top and bottom edges of the reflector so that its sides are about 50 cm. tall and so that the bottom edge will fit snugly around the outside of a coffee can and end in a circular edge at the can's base. With masking tape, tape the sides of the reflector so that it will not unroll. Then set it aside until the heating chamber is ready.

Using metal shears, trim down the sides of the coffee can to a height of 6 cm., leaving two 3-cm. tabs opposite each other at the top edge. Bind the cut edges with masking tape, and paint all tape and metal surfaces with flat black paint. When the paint has dried, glue the can to a styrofoam block, about 3 cm. by 8 cm. by 20 cm. Place the reflector over the can once more so that the trimmed lower edge of the reflector rests flat on the surface of the block of styrofoam. Press the metal tabs against the sides of the reflector for a snug fit. Then point the reflector toward the sun, propping it in a box to support it in the desired position, as shown in Figure 8-1. Place some food to be heated, such as a foil-wrapped Danish pastry (sweet roll) with an outer covering of black contruction paper, in the can, and place an inverted glass bowl over the can. After about 15 minutes remove and unwrap the food—and enjoy your heated Danish!

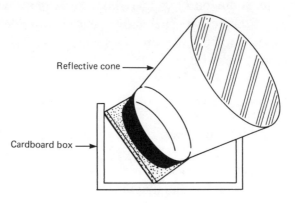

Figure 8-1. Design for a solar oven

ACTIVITY: MAKING A PLASTIC-BAG GREENHOUSE

Place a clear plastic garment bag of the type used by dry cleaners over a house plant in a hanging planter. Gather the plastic around the top center to close the opening, and tape it to the hanger. Next, gather the plastic at the lower end, twisting it until a loose knot can be tied, thus closing the bottom end also. Hang the plant in an area of moderate heat and light to tide it over a weekend or school vacation period when no personal care can be given. Similarly cover plants in regular planters with plastic bags that can be taped and tied closed, thus fashioning for each an individual greenhouse. Plants treated in this manner thrive in their individual greenhouses until the vacation period is over.

ACTIVITY: MAKING A PERISCOPE

Carefully cut off the tops of two clean milk cartons. On one side of one carton measure and mark a 45° angle from one bottom corner to the side opposite. Repeat this procedure on the opposite side of the carton so that both lines are even with each other. Prepare the second carton in an identical manner. Then, using a razor blade, make a slit along all four lines drawn. Slide a rectangular mirror, shiny surface facing up toward the open end of the carton, into each carton so that each mirror fits between a pair of slits which support it in this position.

Now, in one side of each carton, cut out a circular porthole, directly opposite the reflecting surface of the installed mirror. Fit the two cartons together, placing the open end of one over the open end of the other so that the circular holes face in opposite directions, and tape the cartons together along the seam where they are joined together. The periscope, as shown in Figure 8-2, is constructed to change the direction of light by

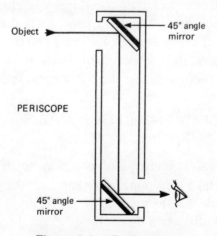

Figure 8-2. Periscope

reflecting it twice, both times through an angle of 90°. It may be used to view objects in the same manner that is found to be effective by submarine crews.

SCIENCE ACTIVITIES RELATING TO
EFFECTIVE WAYS OF DOING THINGS

Students enjoy engaging in activities that provide them with opportunities to put scientific information to some practical use. They find that learning about ways to do things more effectively is a stimulating experience; after the completion of an activity which focuses on a scientific procedure applied to a specific situation, they often raise questions about additional applications to other situations.

Of course, the use of some procedures is not new to them. They all have had experience with some procedures practiced as a matter of routine. But activities designed to encourage them to delve into the reasons *why* these procedures are used and *why* they work as they do satisfies student curiosity and gives meaning and purpose to the procedures while dignifying them with a proper justification. A sampling of activities of this type involving representative topics and procedures will elicit interest and activity in many more. What is important is that students become aware of the importance of science and its applications to practical matters that affect their lives in a multitude of ways—and to recognize that the list is constantly growing.

ACTIVITY: PROPAGATING HOUSE PLANTS
FROM CUTTINGS

Select a healthy house plant such as *Swedish ivy* or *begonia* from which to take a cutting. Make sure that the plant is strong and vigorous and that the piece to be cut off is young and tender. Using a sharp knife, cut a shoot about 7.5 cm. long from the end of a stem, cutting it neatly directly beneath the spot where a leaf appears. Then carefully trim off all leaves on the lower third of the shoot.

Fill a suitably-sized glass jar with fresh cold water and place the cutting in it so that the bottom third of the stem is under water. Several cuttings may be placed in the same jar if care is taken to avoid overcrowding. Place the jar out of direct sunlight, but in an area that does provide sufficient light. Check the water level in the jar every few days, adding water as needed to replace that which has been used by the plant shoot or lost by evaporation. In about 2-3 weeks roots will begin to appear. When the root growth measures about 2-3 cm. in length, transfer the young plants to flower pots or other planters containing a good potting soil mixture for house plants.

ACTIVITY: FINDING THE VOLUME OF AN IRREGULARLY SHAPED OBJECT

Tie a string around an irregularly shaped object, such as a rock specimen, and obtain a graduated cylinder of suitable size and shape to accommodate the specimen. Pour water into the cylinder until it reaches the 250-ml. level, as read on the lower meniscus. Then, holding the free end of the string to which the specimen is attached, lower the suspended specimen into the water in the cylinder so that the object becomes fully immersed and the water level rises in the cylinder as shown in Figure 8-3. Now determine the volume of the contents of the cylinder. The difference between the two volume readings represents the volume of water displaced by the object which was immersed and therefore the volume of the object.

To measure the volume of an object which is less dense than water, provide an extension of the string around the solid object to which a lead weight can be attached at the lower end. Then, separately measure the amount of water displaced by the weight alone and by the combined object and weight. The difference between the two volumes may be taken as the volume of the object.

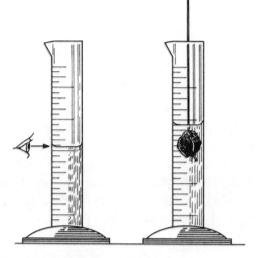

Figure 8-3.   Measuring the volume of an irregularly shaped
object by water displacement

ACTIVITY: DESALTING WATER

Dissolve 5 g. of table salt in 100 ml. of water. Transfer the salt water to a 250-ml. flask and obtain a one-hole rubber stopper which will fit the flask. Into the hole in the stopper insert a short piece of glass tubing which is connected to a 60-cm. length of plastic tubing at its other end. Place the rubber stopper in the neck of the flask, making sure that all connections are tight. Then place the flask on a hot plate so that the tubing extends to a clean glass jar placed about 40 cm. away. Heat the water in the flask, allowing it to boil vigorously. Observe the formation of droplets of moisture in the tubing and the drops of water falling into the jar. Continue the process of heating and collecting until about 50 ml. of water have been collected in the jar. Then touch a clean fingertip first to the ''purified'' water and then to the tip of the tongue and note whether the water tastes salty or if the salt has been left behind in the flask by a process that permits fresh water to be obtained from a salt water source.

ACTIVITY: MAKING CARPETING SAFE
FOR USE IN HOMES

Obtain a small piece of rubber-backed carpeting. At one edge of the carpet attach a bent paper clip, making a hook to which a spring balance can be attached. Position the carpet, backing side down, on a tabletop. Place a heavy book in the center of the carpet and attach a spring balance to the free end of the paper clip hook. Pulling gently on the spring balance, pull the carpet slowly across the table. When the carpet begins to move, read on the spring balance the amount of force needed to overcome inertia and cause the carpet to slide.

For comparison, repeat the procedure using a piece of carpet, similar to the first except that it lacks a rubber backing material. Note the amount of force needed to overcome friction and move this piece of carpeting. Compare the amount of force needed to cause a carpet, with and without rubber backing, to slide. Then determine why rubber-backed carpeting is recommended for use in homes.

ACTIVITY: DETERMINING HOW MANY
SEEDS WILL GROW

Fold a square meter of muslin cloth twice in the same direction. Wet the cloth and lay it lengthwise on a table. Then select a sample of one hundred unbroken specimens from a batch of seeds whose viability, or ability to grow, is to be tested. Arrange the seeds in rows, 2 cm. apart, on the top half of the muslin strip. Fold the bottom half of the muslin up so that it covers the seeds. Then roll up the double layer loosely, but without allowing any of the seeds to become dislodged. Tie string around the roll in three places to form a "rag-doll-tester."

Keep the tester moist and warm for several days, checking daily to see if the seeds have sprouted. When the seeds have germinated unroll the muslin and count the number of seeds that have sprouted. Record this number as a percentage; for example, if eighty-four out of the one hundred seeds tested were observed to sprout, the viability of the seeds in the batch is 84 percent. If fewer seeds are tested, calculate the *percentage* of viable seeds in the sample. This percentage of the remaining seeds in the packet may be expected to germinate successfully and produce plants.

ACTIVITY: DISTINGUISHING A RAW EGG
FROM A HARD-BOILED EGG

Obtain two fresh eggs of the same size. Place one in boiling water and cook it for 15 minutes or until it becomes hard-boiled. After it has been removed from the boiling water and allowed to cool down to room temperature, make a pencil mark on one side of the eggshell to identify it. Similarly identify the uncooked egg, also at room temperature, with a distinguishing mark.

Place both eggs on a platter, identifying marks facing down, and set them into a spinning motion. Observe the manner and time of their spinning. Due to the inertia of the fluid within the raw egg, the egg which has not been cooked will be the first to stop spinning. The hard-boiled egg will be observed to spin for a longer time.

ACTIVITY: INVESTIGATING THE EFFECTIVENESS
OF INSULATION

Obtain permission to use an oven in a classroom setting where the teacher can supervise the handling of hot objects and materials in a manner which emphasizes the importance of taking all safety precautions. If no classroom oven is available, one located at home or in the school lunchroom or cooking room may be used if a responsible adult is present to enforce strict adherence to all rules that would ensure student safety.

Obtain two oven thermometers. Place one thermometer in a covered baking dish, and completely wrap the covered dish with a fireproof insulating material. Place the insulated dish and the other, uncovered, thermometer side by side in an oven that has been preheated to 175° C. Allow them to remain in the heated oven for 10 minutes. Then, using safety mitts to avoid burning the hands, remove the insulated dish from the oven, quickly remove the insulating material, open the dish, and observe the temperature reading as recorded on the enclosed thermometer. Working quickly, also remove the other thermometer from the oven and read the temperature indicated.

After comparing the readings representative of the temperature in the interior and on the outside of the insulated dish while in the heated oven, determine the effectiveness of insulating materials used to modify the temperature of a closed system.

ACTIVITY: MAKING PLANTS BUSHIER

Obtain a healthy young potted house plant, such as a *Coleus*, that is growing vigorously. Pinch off the growing tip at the top of the stem and dab the stump with an auxin paste. Each time new growth appears near this tip, repeat the procedure, continuing the treatment for several weeks while maintaining the plant in favorable growing conditions. Observe the change in the plant's appearance as it becomes sturdy and bushy. Then compare this shape and appearance with that of a similar plant which had not been given the "pinch and dab of auxin" treatment.

ACTIVITY: INVESTIGATING THE EFFECTIVENESS OF SMELLING SALTS

Carefully pour a small amount of household ammonia into a clean glass jar. Then, with the teacher present to supervise the activity, use the following procedure for "whiffing" chemical vapors in a safe manner: with one hand hold the jar about 20 cm. from your nose at a height that will permit your other hand to move freely above the open jar without coming in contact with either the jar or your face. Using your free hand to produce a fanning motion, direct some vapors from the open jar toward your nose, taking care to avoid holding the jar directly under your nose or inhaling the vapors from the substance in the jar. Notice the distinctive odor of the vapors whiffed in this manner. Then repeat the procedure using a small container of commercially prepared smelling salts and suggest how and why smelling salts can be used effectively and safely to revive a person who has fainted.

Activities which focus on practical applications of science have a strong impact on elementary school students. Without having any hands-on experience with activities that allow them to explore the importance of scientific knowledge and its usefulness in practical situations, they would be quite unprepared for life in the world today. Engaging in activities that focus on this experience acquaints them with applications of science as a dynamic process and a key factor in science education.

9

Activities for Engaging in Individual and Group Projects

When students are given more freedom to choose activities in which they wish to engage they tend to develop an in-depth knowledge and understanding of the particular phases of science they have selected. This is but one of the advantages that derive from science projects that students are allowed to choose freely. By engaging in activities of this type they are also (1) afforded opportunities to strengthen their use and understanding of the scientific approach, (2) provided a means of acquiring additional practice in skills previously employed, (3) encouraged to communicate their enthusiasm and understanding of what they have learned, and (4) rewarded for their efforts by a sense of pride in what they have accomplished.

For this to occur, project activities should be enjoyable, satisfying, worthwhile, and challenging experiences. They must be carefully selected and planned, with support and guidance supplied, as needed, to ensure that all will be successful. That each student experience success is crucial to the science project program; it encourages the development of positive attitudes toward science and future project work that may be required at a higher grade level, and it promotes a feeling of self-confidence that encourages the use of investigative methods for students to learn on their own.

Projects may take many forms, but all imply something tangible which students can display with pride, possibly at a school exhibit or a science fair. The fact that elementary school students are not equipped to engage in research procedures, of course, imposes some limitations on what might be considered appropriate. In most cases it has been found that projects of the *demonstration* type are the most suitable for elementary science.

Guidelines for Preparing a Project

Although previous activities may suggest some topics and patterns which are suitable, a list of guidelines specifically developed for projects will also be helpful for student reference. Guidelines that provide for student input and for full discussion prior to embarking on the project activities usually produce the best results.

Guidelines for Students Preparing a Project

- Select a topic that interests you and that you think will be of interest to others.
- Remember the topics and procedures that were the most impressive in other activities and include some that might be appropriate.
- Plan your project carefully.
- Keep your project design simple.
- Keep records of all pertinent information gathered from reading and investigative work.
- Seek help, when needed, but DO YOUR OWN WORK and DO NOT EXPECT A READY-MADE PROJECT.
- Employ all safety precautions applicable to your "experimental" work.
- Allow yourself ample time to complete all aspects of the project, including the display.
- Keep the display or exhibit uncluttered.
- Be sure you understand your project thoroughly.

Whether the project evolves as an extension of an open-ended activity engaged in at an earlier date or is being pursued in a new area, there is a built-in freedom for choosing and developing the project that allows students to make it highly individualized. It then becomes a true expression of the individual or group that prepared it.

PROJECTS THAT SIMULATE NATURAL OCCURRENCES

Capturing the true representation of a natural phenomenon can be accomplished more effectively by a model than by pictures or word descriptions. While referring to pictures and reference books students have an opportunity to digest the pertinent information and bring meaning to an otherwise inert model. Including essential details, or making a working model that others can operate gives evidence of the thoroughness with which the student prepared his project. Students who opt for this type of project should be encouraged to research it thoroughly and supply relevant information when preparing their display or exhibit.

PROJECT: MAKING A FOSSIL IMPRINT

Cut a piece of sturdy tagboard to make a rectangular or circular frame with side walls about 5 cm. high. Next add water to plaster of Paris to make a thick mixture. Pour the mixture into the frame, filling it about halfway, and level off the surface of the plaster, making it smooth and even. Next place a coating of petroleum jelly over the surface of a scallop shell or other seashell, and position the shell, curved surface down, on the surface of the wet plaster. Press the shell down into the mixture until the edges of the shell are at the same level as the surface of the plaster mixture. Allow the plaster to dry and harden. In one side wall of the frame punch a small hole that is also level with the surface of the plaster. Then pass a pencil through the hole so that one end of the pencil lays flat against the shell and the other protrudes 2-3 cm. beyond the hole in the side wall. Coat the surface of the hardened plaster with petroleum jelly, and pour a freshly-made plaster mixture on top of the shell, the plaster surface, and the pencil, filling the frame to the top. Level the surface as before, and again allow the plaster to harden. Finally, separate the two plaster layers and carefully remove the pencil and the shell. The top mold shows an *internal* imprint of the shell, while the bottom mold shows its *external* imprint.

To make a cast of the shell, fit the two molds together and hold them in this position with stout elastic bands. Then pour melted crayon wax through the opening and channel made by the pencil, and set the mold aside until the cast sets. Finally, separate the two blocks and carefully remove the ''fossil'' shell.

PROJECT: MAKING A CEMENTED SEDIMENTARY ROCK

Cut down two clean milk cartons to a height of about 10 cm. Use a nail to punch several holes in the sides and bottom of one carton. Then fill the carton one-third full of small washed pebbles of the type used to line the bottom of aquarium tanks. Keep the other carton to be used as a collecting vessel.

In a jar, prepare a mixture consisting of two parts of white glue to one part of water. While holding the perforated carton a few centimeters directly above the collecting vessel, pour the glue-water mixture over the pebbles, collecting the liquid that runs out through the perforations. Wait for 2-3 minutes and repeat the process, using the collected liquid to pour once more over the pebbles. Repeat the process several times, allowing several minutes to elapse between applications and making certain that all pebbles are bathed with the glue-water mixture. Set the carton in a warm place and allow it to remain undisturbed until the next day. Then strip away the sides and bottom of the carton and examine the hardened mass which simulates a sedimentary rock.

PROJECT: MAKING A MODEL VOLCANO

In a cut-down milk carton mix non-asbestos plaster of Paris

and water to make a thick slurry. Tie one end of a 20-cm. length of knitting yarn around a 3-cm. piece of wax broken from a thick wax crayon. Push the crayon piece into the wet plaster, making certain that it is completely surrounded by plaster, but not touching the sides of the carton, and allowing the free end of the yarn to hang over the side of the carton. Then place the carton in a safe location where it may remain undisturbed until the plaster has hardened. When the plaster is dry and hard, snip the yarn close to the surface of the plaster and peel away the sides and bottom of the milk carton. While the teacher or a responsible adult supervises the activity, heat the plaster block directly over the open flame of a bunsen burner until there is some evidence that the crayon is melting. Observe what happens as the crayon melts, and relate this to a volcano in which pressure is built up by the increase in volume resulting from the heating of certain materials within the earth's interior.

PROJECT: MAKING EGGSHELL GEODES

Place 150 ml. of water in a beaker and, while stirring constantly, slowly add copper sulfate crystals. Place the beaker on a hot plate and gently heat the mixture. Continue to stir the mixture as it is being heated, adding more copper sulfate gradually until no more crystals will dissolve. When the saturation point has been reached, remove the beaker from the heat source. While the copper sulfate solution is cooling, carefully clean some eggshell halves. Select several that show no cracks or excessively ragged edges, and set them in an empty egg carton where they can be supported in an upright position. Carefully pour the cooled copper sulfate solution into several eggshells, filling them almost to the brim. Then set the carton aside where the solution-filled shells can remain undisturbed for several days. When sufficient liquid has evaporated and the solution has solidified, examine the crystal formation in the simulated "geodes."

PROJECTS THAT INVOLVE EXPERIMENTS

Students who were intrigued in their earliest science experience by experiments are probably still most attracted to situations in which they investigate to determine the results in a particular situation.

Since elaborate equipment will probably not be available, students must be advised to keep the experimental design of their projects simple. And to check the accuracy of their work they should be encouraged to repeat the experiment to verify the results obtained and reported.

PROJECT: INVESTIGATING PREFERENCES FOR LIGHT INTENSITY AMONG SMALL ANIMALS

Obtain a glass or clear plastic tube which measures about 5 cm. in diameter and 24 cm. in length, and which is equipped with snap-on covers to permit a tight closure at each end. Cut white letter paper into three strips, each 0.5 cm. less in width than the circumference of the tube. Cut the strips individually to produce lengths of 18 cm., 12 cm., and 6 cm., and overlap them to form three regions of different thicknesses, each 6 cm. long. Then, using rubber bands, attach the paper to the tube, leaving a narrow slit along one side where the paper does not quite fit completely around the tube. Orient the paper to form a graduated light intensity pattern from one end of the tube to the other; the triple thickness should be at one end of the tube, followed by the double thickness, then the single thickness, and finally a 6-cm. region which remains uncovered at the opposite end.

Place a fairly large number of specimens of the same species of small animal (*Drosophila*, crayfish, sowbug, ant, or beetle) in the tube and place both caps securely in position. Lay the tube on its side on a table with the viewing slit facing away from the direct light source placed 15 cm. above the tube. Allow the tube to remain in this position for 10 minutes. After 10 minutes have elapsed, use the viewing strip area to determine how many specimens can be counted in each light intensity zone. Return the specimens to their culture chamber and analyze the data collected for light intensity preferences exhibited by the test organisms.

PROJECT: INVESTIGATING SOAP AND SOAP BUBBLES

Using a variety of commercial soap products, prepare a series of soap solutions: for each solution place 15 ml. of a liquid soap or 15 g. of a soap powder in 1000 ml. of hot water, and allow the solution to stand for 2-3 days. Meantime, make bubble blowers from soda straws: use a razor blade to slit one end of each drinking straw into four parts which extend about 1 cm. and can be spread outward. Place the solutions to be tested in separate containers and provide an unused blower for use in each test: first dip the spread end of a prepared straw into a solution being tested; then remove and, pointing the wetted end away from the mouth, blow gently through the untreated end. As each solution is tested examine the bubbles that appear and grow in size. Watch for colors to become visible when each bubble swells, stretching its outer wall as it becomes thinner. Judge the best soap for bubbles on the basis of the size and color of bubbles produced and on the time they last before bursting.

PROJECT: DETERMINING WHAT HAPPENS
WHEN YOU SHAKE SAND

Obtain two paper cups of the same size and shape. Fill one cup one-third full of dry sand. Lower the bulb of a thermometer into the sand and read the temperature in degrees Celsius. Record the temperature reading and remove the thermometer. Invert the second cup over the first and tape the two cups together in this position, using masking tape to join them rim to rim. Shake the cups so that the sand moves back and forth from one cup to the other. Continue the shaking for about 10 minutes. Then poke a hole in the base of the top cup and insert the thermometer down into the sand so that the bulb is submerged. Again, read and record the temperature, and determine if there has been a change in temperature. Explain what has caused any change in temperature that has been detected.

PROJECT: INVESTIGATING THE RESIDUE FROM A SMOKED CIGARETTE

Thoroughly clean and rinse a discarded clear plastic squeeze bottle of the sort used for liquid soap or dishwashing liquid. Insert a short length of glass tubing through a one-hole rubber stopper that fits the bottle opening. Loosely pack the tube with white absorbent cotton, and check to be sure that there are tight connections between the stopper and the bottle.

Place a nonfilter cigarette in the open end of the glass tube and secure its position there. After squeezing the plastic bottle to force the air out, light the cigarette at its free end. Then, alternately press on the sides of the plastic bottle and release the pressure with a rhythmic pumping action that simulates the smoking of a cigarette.

After the cigarette has been completely "smoked," discontinue the regular pumping action and discard the butt. Then carefully remove the cotton from the tube and look for accumulations of tar. Note the color, texture, odor, and amount of the residue collected on the cotton for each of a variety of cigarette brands tested, using a "smoking" bottle such as the one shown in Figure 9-1.

PROJECT: CHECKING A WATER SAMPLE FOR DISSOLVED OXYGEN

Obtain two small glass jars with screw cap tops. Clean the jars thoroughly, and in one jar place a clean pad of steel wool. Fill both jars with tap water, adding two drops of methylene blue solution to each. Fasten the caps securely and allow the jars to remain undisturbed in an area where they can be observed periodically. Note the fading of blue color and the rusting of the

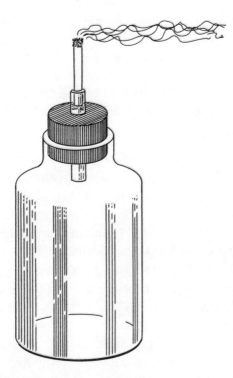

Figure 9-1. A "smoking" bottle

steel wool pad in one jar, while the blue color, in the absence of steel wool, persists in the other. Relate the blue color of the dye to the presence of dissolved oxygen, which, if removed to take part in the formation of rust, causes the color of the methylene blue solution to fade.

PROJECT: CHECKING THE VALUE OF NATURAL SELTZER WATER FOR PLANT GROWTH

Obtain two house plants of the same variety and of similar size, shape, and state of health. Water one in the normal way, using aged tap water for the watering treatments. Water and mist the experimental plant with natural seltzer water containing carbon dioxide. Be sure not to use club soda which contains some salts as well. Apply the seltzer water about once every 10 days, and, after a time, compare the experimental plant with the control. On the basis of the comparison evaluate the advertising claim that natural seltzer water is "excellent for house plants."

PROJECT: CHECKING THE VALUE OF GELATIN AS A PLANT GROWTH SUBSTANCE

Obtain two house plants of the same variety and of similar size, shape, and state of health. Designate one of the plants as "experimental" to receive applications of a gelatin mixture prepared in the following manner: dissolve one envelope of unflavored gelatin in 250 ml. of hot tap water and add 750 ml. of cold water to make 1 l. of the mixture. Once a month, using a freshly prepared mixture, use the gelatin mixture as part of the normal watering and feeding pattern of the experimental plant. Between applications of the mixture to the experimental plant, provide both plants with identical conditions of heat, light, watering, and feeding which are known to favor their growth. After a 3- or 4-month experimental period, compare the two plants. On the basis of the comparison evaluate the advertising claim that house plants appear "fuller, greener, and healthier" when nourished with a rich supply of nitrogen available from the gelatin source.

PROJECTS THAT INVOLVE MAKING AND CONSTRUCTING THINGS

Making things out of simple materials appeals to the creative instincts of students. They are often amazed at how easy it is to construct a simple form of an object or a mechanism which in its manufactured form looks awesome, yet is taken for granted. Although the end result is the finished product, the real value of the project comes from the construction and the accompanying understanding of how the object works—and being able to explain to others the role of science that made it possible.

PROJECT: MAKING A BOTTLED ECOSYSTEM

A miniature ecosystem can be created in a large bottle or a wide-mouth glass jar that has been thoroughly cleaned. Add a layer of crushed rock or pebbles to the bottom of the jar and then a layer of sand and soil. Add enough pond water to fill the jar to a height that allows for an air space above the water level. Allow the water to settle for about 3 days or until the water has cleared. Then, after anchoring some small water plants, add some small fish and snails.

Place the mini-ecosystem in a location which provides indirect sunlight and a moderate room temperature. When the plants and animals all appear to be healthy and thriving, stopper the bottle or jar and allow the enclosed ecosystem, now balanced, to exist as a miniature balance of nature.

PROJECT: MAKING A STRING TELEPHONE

Punch a small hole in the bottom of each of two paper cups of the same size. Thread a string, approximately 60 cm. in length, through these holes and knot the ends inside the cups. Stretch the string taut across the distance between the "mouth-piece" and the "receiver," taking care to prevent anything from touching the string and damping the vibrations. Hold one cup close to your mouth and talk into it while a friend holds the other cup close to his ear and listens. Then reverse the procedure so that you can receive a reply from the person at the other end of the line.

PROJECT: MAKING LEAF IMPRINTS

Grease a paper plate and set it aside. In a plastic bowl mix water with some non-asbestos plaster of Paris to make a mixture that has the consistency of cake batter. Add a pinch of salt and stir it into the mixture. Then pour the mixture into the greased plate. Position several undamaged leaves on the surface of the wet mixture, pressing them firmly against the plaster so that contact is made at all points. Allow the plaster to dry and set. Then, carefully remove the leaves and examine the imprints which show the leaf outlines and the vein patterns within them. To make a hanging display, remove the dried plaster from the paper plate and attach a hook to the back of the plaster.

PROJECTS THAT CONCERN LIVING THINGS

Raising, watching, and caring for plants and animals is an interest that is common among elementary school students. Responsibility for the success of living things in their care demands constant monitoring that focuses on the requirements for life and for the activities in which they engage. It often involves providing special conditions and accommodations as well. Through their involvement in projects of this type, students increase their understanding of life and of living and develop a kinship with all things that live, be they plant or animal.

PROJECT: INVESTIGATING REGENERATION IN PLANARIANS

Collect planarians from a fresh water brook and select some specimens that are well-formed and undamaged. Place a planarian in a small dish of pond water. Using a razor blade, cut the worm into two pieces across the middle to make a tail piece and a head piece. Use another planarian in another dish to cut in the opposite way, making a left half and a right half. (See Figure 9-2). Label the dishes and place them in a cool spot. Make a diagram of the appearance of the cut worms and record the date. Then maintain the dishes in a cool, dark area and, using a hand lens, make daily observations, replenishing the water supply if needed. After about 2 weeks you will have four planarians, because the planarian can grow a whole new body from one part that remains after an injury or an accidental or intentional separation of its body into two parts.

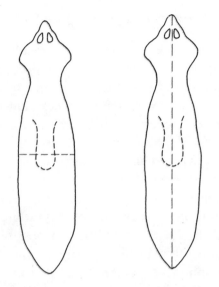

Figure 9-2.   Regeneration in Planarians

PROJECT: HATCHING BRINE SHRIMP

Thoroughly wash and rinse a wide-mouth jar, such as a large pickle jar. Fill the jar to within 8 cm. of the top with natural sea water or with a salt solution made by dissolving 12 g. of non-iodized salt in 4 1. of pond water. Add 1.5 g. of brine shrimp eggs to the liquid and wet them thoroughly by gentle stirring. Attach the glass pipette from a medicine dropper to the end of an air line hose which is also attached to an air pump. Lower the pipette into the jar and supply sufficient air pressure to create top-to-bottom circulation within the water in the jar. Maintain the hatchery in a location that provides conditions of moderate light and a temperature between 20° C. and 30° C. After 24-48 hours observe the larvae that have hatched. Then supply them with appropriate food such as a freshly-prepared suspension of yeast in fresh water floated on the surface of the liquid.

PROJECT: CHECKING OUT A BIONIC INSECT

Locate an area where earwigs may be hiding and capture some specimens, transferring them to a collecting jar with air holes. Chill the insects by placing the jar in a bowl of crushed ice for 10-15 minutes. When the specimens have become immobilized, select one for use. With silk thread make a harness to fit over the thorax of the specimen. At the opposite end of the thread attach a small box or a toy automobile or railway car. Then, when they are assembled, place them on a smooth table top and encourage the earwig to move forward, pulling the load behind it. Observe the activity and note the difference in size of the earwig and the load it is pulling. If possible, weigh the earwig and the load. It may be surprising to find that an earwig can pull a load up to five hundred times its own weight.

PROJECT: FINDING PLANTS AND ANIMALS
THAT LIVE IN THE SOIL

Select an area in a garden, a forested area, an empty lot, or a beach from which a 5 cm. by 5 cm. by 5 cm. ground sample can be taken and transferred to a plastic bag. Spread the sample on a large piece of white paper or toweling placed in a large shallow tray and set up a series of paper cups for sorting out the organisms found in the sample. Examine the sample as follows:

Sort out different kinds of living things, putting them in paper cups, labeled by category. Sort out earthworms, sowbugs, slugs, insect larvae and pupae, and other organisms. Provide a paper cup for each kind of organism and count the number of each kind and the total number of organisms that occupied this small amount of soil. Then transfer some of the soil collected to a flowerpot, water the soil, and place it in a warm location. Keep it warm and moist for 1-2 weeks and observe to determine if any plants begin to grow from seeds that may have been present in the soil sample.

PROJECT: GROWING A FLOWERPOT HERB GARDEN

Obtain one or more packets of seeds for growing herbs such as basil, thyme, marjoram, sage, mint, or oregano. Also obtain as many shallow containers as there are kinds of seeds to be grown. Flowerpots with drainage holes or cut-down milk cartons with holes punched in the bottom may be used. Cover the drainage holes with pieces of broken flowerpot or gravel and fill the containers to within 1 cm. of the top with a potting mixture made of equal parts of garden soil, peat moss, and sand. Water the soil well and allow it to drain. When the soil packs down, refill the pots to the proper level. Sow about fifteen seeds per pot, spacing them approximately 1 cm. apart. Then sift soil mixture over the seeds to cover them lightly. Place a plastic bag over each pot and hold it securely in position with a tight rubber band. Maintain the pots in a shallow tray in a protected location where the temperature does not fall below 16° C. at night nor rise above 21° C. in the daytime.

Observe the pots daily until the seeds sprout in about 6 days to 4 weeks, according to the type of plant. When the sprouts are 1 cm. high, remove the plastic bag and place the pots on a shallow tray in a sunny window. Keep the soil slightly moist and well-drained. When there are two pairs of leaves on the seedlings in a pot, prepare to transplant them to a permanent growing chamber. Prepare pots and soil as before. Then transplant the seedlings, individually, keeping a good ball of soil around each root system. In the new planting medium, make a hole that is large enough for the balled root, insert the ball, and press the soil firmly around the transplanted roots. Maintain as before—moist, warm, and in a sunny window. Observe daily and within 4-5 weeks leaves will be ready for harvesting.

PROJECT: OBSERVING AN ANT COLONY

Locate an ant hill and transfer it to a collecting bucket in which it can be transported to the classroom. Later, in an open area, examine the collected material to ascertain the presence of a queen, without whom the colony will not function. Identify the queen by her twice-average size and prepare to transfer her and some of the collected material to a ready and waiting *formicarium* or ant-watching habitat. One design that provides for viewing from two sides and is equipped with both a feeding station and removable opaque doors can be constructed easily, using simple materials and the following directions.

Obtain two squares of glass and two squares of heavy, dark-colored cardboard, each about 30 cm. by 30 cm. Cut a length of 2-cm. by 6-cm. wood into strips, which when fitted together will form a frame for holding the glass pieces securely in an upright position, one 6 cm. behind the other. Leaving one side open for introducing the nesting materials and occupants, assemble the other three sides of the frame around the front and back glass panels. Using masking tape, bind the glass and wood together. Then prepare the fourth side, which will serve as the top of the formicarium: drill two holes, each for accommodating the insertion of a medicine dropper, spaced about 10 cm. apart along the top. Make all necessary adjustments to ensure that the top will fit snugly and evenly when the frame is complete; but do not attach this piece until the nest is occupied. Transfer the queen by aspirator along with about fifty workers and a quantity of collected nesting material to the formicarium. Then enclose the frame by putting the top piece into position, plugging the holes with medicine droppers, and taping all seams securely. Cut four 5-cm. strips of masking tape for attaching the cardboard doors over the glass front and/or back, when desired.

After the watching habitat has been assembled and occupied, as shown in Figure 9-3, observe the colony as it prepares its nest. Tunneling, carrying of soil particles and debris, and the eventual formation of chambers at different depths along the network of tunnels are easily observed through the

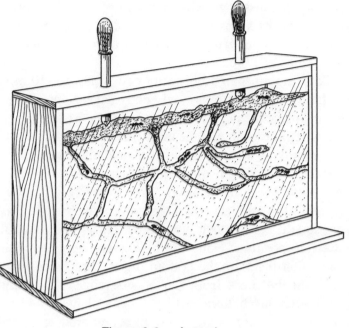

Figure 9-3. Ant colony

glass walls. Look for visible signs of a caste system operating within the colony and identify the specific tasks and maintenance chores being performed. Note also the size of the loads being carried by worker ants.

As a colony becomes established, set up a feeding regimen and observe closely the feeding habits of ants who stand on their hind legs to accept the sugar-water being dispensed by medicine dropper at the feeding station. When you are not viewing, simulate the darkened conditions of an underground habitat by replacing the opaque doors, removing them only when activities of the occupants are to be observed.

PROJECT: MAKING A PANSY GARDEN IN A BASKET

Obtain a collapsible wire mesh hanging vegetable basket of any standard size, from 20 cm. to 30 cm. in diameter. Locate an area where moss is growing luxuriantly and carefully cut out enought sod-like strips to line the basket. Also obtain young pansy plants in sufficient number to cover the basket completely, sides and top.

Soak the moss in a bucket of cool water for 10 minutes. Then take a square of moss and gently squeeze out the excess water and place the moss in the bottom of the basket, green side down. Continue arranging the moss pieces, taking one square at a time, removing the excess moisture, and lining the sides of the basket thickly. Press the moss against the wire frame so that the green moss covers and protrudes over the wire in the bottom, along the sides, and around the top edge of the basket. The wire frame should be completely covered and all moss should be securely in position. Hang the basket and begin to plant the pansies. Starting from the bottom, insert some roots of young plants into the moss from the outside edge, all around the basket. After the bottom level has been planted, add a good potting soil mixture to the center to accommodate all roots at this level. Proceed to the next level, and similarly anchor the roots of young plants and provide potting soil, repeating the process until the basket is planted from bottom to top. Mist the entire planting all over, and hang the basket in a shady location for at least 1 day. Then transfer it to a sunny location that will provide the proper lighting and temperature needed for pansy plants. Mist the entire planting well, and then water daily until all plants have become established and begin to show signs of growth. Maintain the basket garden by providing biweekly applications of concentrated plant food and by maintaining the proper moisture level with a daily watering and misting schedule.

PROJECTS THAT CAN BE PERFORMED
BY GROUPS

Some projects are of general interest and can be performed as a group endeavor. When this is done there should be some responsibility assigned to each student or team so that all can have a vested interest in the performance and completion of the project. Since this type of project usually has long-range values, it is often a bond that ties together members of a class as they plan to reunite after a period of time to check up on the result of their endeavor. Projects of this type should be stimulating as a common experience that is long-lived and that can be continued for an extended period of time.

PROJECT: MAKING A DRIFT BOTTLE

Write a short message on a piece of paper that can be rolled up and placed in a plastic tube that is waterproof. Insert the tube inside a small bottle, filling the bottle with water and stoppering it tightly. Place the bottle in a tub of water and note how rapidly it sinks to the bottom. Then remove the bottle, repeatedly pouring off a small amount of water and testing it each time until it just floats when submerged, as shown in Figure 9-4. If the bottle is to be used in the ocean, test it in salt water. Then set the bottle adrift. Be sure to include the date and a message to the finder about how to contact you or your class when the bottle is found. From the date and location where it is picked up, the direction and speed of the current can be calculated. By its precise weighting the bottle floats just beneath the surface where it is affected by the speed and direction of the current, but remains unaffected by the winds.

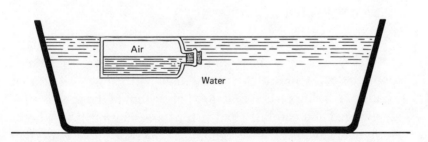

Figure 9-4.   A drift bottle floats just below surface of the water.

PROJECT: MAKING A SCIENCE TIME CAPSULE

Obtain a metal can that it is possible to seal. Thoroughly clean the can and make a decision concerning the items of a scientific nature you and your classmates would like to bury, with plans for the container to be dug up at some time in the future as a record of the science activities that were engaged in by your class. Among those things that might be considered are a setup of a favorite experiment such as one involving air pressure, a demonstration such as "dancing mothballs," or a collection of insects, rocks, fossils, or seashells.

Clean the container thoroughly, inside and out. Paint its interior and its cover with a rust-inhibitor paint and line the inside completely with heavy aluminum foil. Similarly, paint the outside of the container with several coats of the rust inhibitor. Carefully wrap each item to be included, using aluminum foil and boxes, as needed, and place them carefully in the time capsule. Place the lid on the container and seal it with a liquid sealant material. Then give the entire capsule several more applications of the sealant.

Select a location and obtain permission from the school authorities for burying the capsule and marking it on the site and in the official school records. Set a date for digging up the capsule—graduation day, next school year in May to mark its first anniversary, or a date in the future when others may be the ones to examine the science articles that you have buried.

PROJECT: PLANTING A "CLASS" TREE

Obtain permission for planting a tree on schoolgrounds, preferably in a location within viewing distance of the classroom. Select a tree of a species that will grow well in that location, making certain that the root system of the specimen is undamaged and carefully balled for transplanting. Dig a hole, amply wide and deep to accommodate the roots, and set the ball in the hole. Cover the ball, filling in the remaining space in the hole with good soil—acid soil for an evergreen tree, limed compost for all other—and packing the soil well around the roots. Water the area thoroughly, saturating the earth around the roots, and, if necessary, support the tree with stakes and guy wires. Then, to maintain the desired degree of moistness, mulch the newly planted tree with grass cuttings and set up a schedule for watering the roots and spraying the above-ground growth with water. Make long-term plans for continued observation of the tree, at specific times such as an anniversary date of its planting, Arbor Day of the next school year, and the class graduation day.

Science projects are perhaps the single most important activity for encouraging students to explore things of a *scientific* nature in a *scientific* way. They may be as varied as the students who undertake them, and will certainly be helpful in identifying those who are scientifically talented. The main value, however, comes from the impact the involvement has on each student as an individual. The success he experiences, the satisfaction he derives, and the recognition he receives relative to his accomplishment will contribute significantly in molding his developing attitude toward science.

10

Activities for Participating in Science Experiences for Fun and Enjoyment

It seems fitting that, as each school year draws to a close, students should be provided with opportunities to engage in activities that review some of the important aspects and applications of the science they have learned. For this to be effective, the activities need to be designed to present the review material in a context different from the initial exposure and with a mild challenge for students to make the association and identification as the material applies to the new situation. This time around, however, the emphasis on *fun with science* offers strong motivation for reinforcing learning and understanding by participation in what are definitely change-of-pace activities.

Games, puzzles, races, competitions, toys, mysteries, and illusions—all lend an air of excitement to the activities which may be designed for individuals, groups, or an entire class. Each activity should recall to the participant some scientific information of importance, and the successful completion of each activity should be a personally satisfying experience for the individual involved. Many activities may look ahead to the summer vacation period and beyond, some suggesting leisure-time activities for individuals to employ to entertain themselves or their friends, and others encouraging a sustained interest in a topic with the potential for developing into a summer or a life-long hobby.

Recognition of the importance of scientific materials is in evidence in the multitude of sophisticated toys, games, and puzzles which are designed for people of all ages and which are marketed widely and successfully. Their educational impact is also significant in that many of these materials can be used to dramatize a particular situation or to help students gain an insight more clearly than was possible using more conventional instructional devices. However, care must be taken in their selection, with special precautions to avoid materials which are too complex or in which the presentation of scientific information is misleading or obscured, due to the high priority rating assigned to giving the product a more marketable popular appeal.

In most cases homemade materials are best suited for science activities. Indeed, the involvement of students in the preparation of the materials is a valuable part of their learning. It is the rewards and pleasures, however, which offer strong incentive and enjoyable experiences that enhance the learning potential of these activities—and through participation in these "windup" activities the retention of scientific ideas may be broadened considerably.

ACTIVITIES INVOLVING FUN WITH TOYS

Scientific toys have been known and used for over 2,000 years. One of the earliest, the *Ball of Winds,* made by Hero in ancient Alexandria, fascinated the children of that day in much the same way that modern scientific toys attract and amuse today's students.

The destructiveness observed in children who take apart a toy is often an expression of their interest in learning how it works. By providing them with activities that involve playing with toys which they have made themselves, they will be afforded an intimate knowledge of the construction *without* the necessity of taking them apart. This aspect of their curiosity satisfied, the activity can continue, stimulating them to learn the scientific principles that are involved.

Of course, toys are fun objects and the activities which employ them will be most effective if presented in a fun way, albeit educational as well.

ACTIVITY: SPINNING A FRISBEE GYROSCOPE

Drive a hole in the center of a frisbee. Then push a pencil through the hole so that the pencil and the frisbee are at right angles to each other. Holding the pencil in an upright position, as shown in Figure 10-1, spin it like a top. Observe that as the pencil spins the frisbee rotates around the pencil, making a toy gyroscope. See how long your gyroscope will continue to spin and note that when it is not spinning or rotating it topples over.

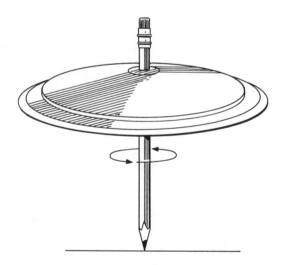

Figure 10-1.   A gyroscope made from a frisbee and a pencil

ACTIVITY: OBSERVING A HEAT-DRIVEN PINWHEEL

Make a pinwheel by cutting a 7.5-cm. square of aluminum foil diagonally from each corner to within 1 cm. of the center. Fold back every other point to the center of the square, and insert a straight pin through these corners, then through the center, and finally into an eraser at the top of a pencil. Using the pencil as a handle, hold the pinwheel a few centimeters directly above a heat source such as a hot plate or a radiator. As the warmed air expands and rises, it pushes against the blades of the pinwheel. This causes the pinwheel to turn.

ACTIVITY: FLOATING WALNUT-SHELL BARGES

Prepare three or more walnut-shell barges in the following manner: with melted paraffin attach one-half of a small cork to each end of a cleaned-out half of a walnut shell so that (1) the top of the cork will be level with the top of the shell and (2) each cork will form a flat vertical surface when the barges are floated on water.

Float the walnut-shell barges individually on water in a large tub. Then line them up end to end. Holding a stick in front of the first barge in the chain, pull the entire chain of barges across the water in the tub by pulling the stick slowly through the water.

Attach a small piece of soap to another stick and observe that when it is placed in water it repels a barge. Using both sticks simultaneously, holding one in each hand, make the barges engage in some interesting maneuvers, such as negotiating forward and/or backward motion singly or in groups, and joining or leaving a chain formation involving three or more units. This may mystify your friends and classmates until you explain to them the weakening effect of soap on the force of attraction associated with the film on water at its surface.

ACTIVITY: MAKING A MODEL
OF AN ANCIENT STEAM TOY

Thoroughly clean a small tin can such as a wax or paint can that is equipped with a snap-in metal top. Drive into the sides of the can two holes large enough to accommodate one-hole rubber stoppers, the holes being positioned on opposite sides of the can. Obtain two pieces of glass tubing of suitable diameter to fit into the one-hole stoppers and bend each to form an elbow curve with one end drawn to form a jet. Then fit the glass tubes into the stoppers and insert the stoppers into the holes in the can so that the jets are on the outside, both facing in the same direction. Pour water into the can to a depth of about 3 cm. and place the cover securely into position. Check all fittings to be sure they are tight. Tie the ends of a 60-cm. length of cord to the stoppers and suspend the entire assembly from a chain as shown in Figure 10-2.

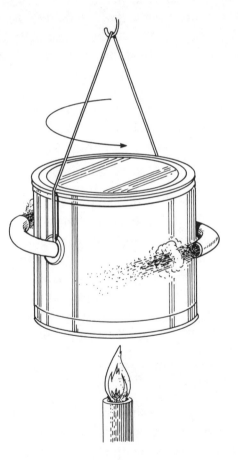

Figure 10-2.   Model of Hero's steam toy

With a teacher present to supervise the activity, place the can over a bunsen burner flame and observe your model in action. It is a model of a steam toy made centuries ago in ancient Egypt.

ACTIVITY: MAKING MUSIC WITH DRINKING STRAWS

Flatten a 1-cm. segment at one end of a paper drinking straw. With scissors cut a small triangular wedge out of each side of this flattened segment to make a mouthpiece that resembles the reed of a clarinet or other reed musical instrument.

Place the mouthpiece in your mouth with the flattened portion held just back of your lips. Blow hard through the straw and note the sound produced. In a similar manner make a series of straws of various lengths and arrange them from longest to shortest to determine the pitch that each produces. Then enlist the help of a few friends and orchestrate your musical version of a popular tune or a school song.

ACTIVITY: HOLDING A MAGNETIC BOAT RACE

Fold a sheet of paper to make a paper boat about 10 cm. long. Then magnetize a large darning needle by stroking it with a magnet. Lay the magnetized needle diagonally from the top of one end of the boat to a point near the center of the base.

Prepare four cork floats—flat corks tied to lead weights—to mark off the racecourse. Anchor the floats at equal distances around a tub of water with enough space between each float and the outer rim of the tub to accommodate the boat when moving. Then place the boat at the starting float and, using a magnet, direct the boat completely around the course marked off by the floats. Record the time that is required for the boat to complete the course.

When conducting a race, have each contestant magnetize his own needle but use the same magnet, boat, and racecourse. The contestant who runs the boat from the starting point to the finish line in the shortest time shall be proclaimed the winner.

To inject an element of keener competition into the races, a meet may be held at a later date when contestants may enter individually designed and constructed boats. The enthusiasm engendered by the more competitive approach encourages students to probe more deeply for an understanding and application of the scientific principles involved as they find great fun and excitement in the sport of ''magnetic boat racing.''

ACTIVITY: BLASTING OFF A TOY ROCKET

Thread one end of a 10-m. cord through a small plastic drinking straw. Attach one end of the cord to a hook near a shelf or window fixture at a relatively high elevation. Then stretch the cord to the opposite side of the room, sliding the straw along to keep it within easy reach. Pull the cord taut and attach it to a chair or table so that it forms an inclined pathway from one end of the room to the other with no obstructions. Now inflate a long balloon until its shape is smooth and there is no bump on its end. Twist the neck of the balloon to prevent air from escaping, and slide a large paper clip over the twisted neck.

Position the balloon in contact with the plastic straw so that the balloon and straw are touching and the smooth end of the balloon is facing up the incline made by the cord. Using two 5-cm. strips of masking tape for the purpose, tape the balloon and the straw together. Position the balloon close to the chair and check to be sure that the cord is still taut. (See Figure 10-3.) Holding the balloon in this position begin the countdown. At *blastoff* slide the paper clip off the twisted end of the balloon and let it go. Then watch the rocket as it whooshes along the cord.

ACTIVITY: SAILING A L'EGGS BOAT

Obtain a 10-cm. circular wooden lollipop stick to serve as a sailboat mast. Also obtain a piece of plastic adhesive-backed paper, such as Con-Tact, from which to cut two triangular sails that measure 8 cm. on each side. Remove the backing from the paper sails and glue them together, back-to-back, with the

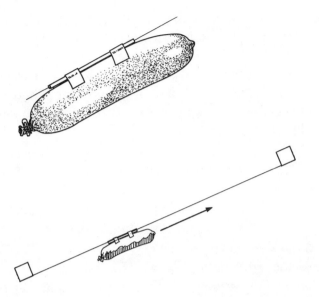

Figure 10-3. A toy rocket

lollipop stick mast between them so that the tip of the mast is even with one point of the triangle of the sail. Then apply glue to the free end of the mast and glue it in an upright position to the inside base of the smaller portion of an empty L'EGGS panty-hose container. Allow the glue to dry thoroughly so that the mast and sails are secure. When completely dry, enjoy sailing the "egg-boat" on water.

ACTIVITIES INVOLVING SCIENTIFIC GAMES

"Fun and Games" activities occupy a prominent place among other activities in science. Because students naturally like games and can learn effectively from them, the inclusion of game forms which enrich the science program is amply justified. Although science games have great value for increasing student interest in the field and in strengthening and facilitating learning in a specific area, their use during the final month of the school year is primarily directed toward reviewing certain aspects of topics that have been a part of the program of learning.

There are many games designed for small groups which are available commercially, and students can be encouraged to develop more, adapting some of the popular patterns and designs to selected topics in science. The learning that results is twofold:

1. Students learn while researching the accuracy of information to be included in the game they are designing.
2. Students learn while participating in the game, profiting in each go-round by having wrong responses corrected.

Games provide a good way for students to learn and to reinforce their learning—and to have fun while doing it.

ACTIVITY: CONDUCTING A SCIENCE TREASURE HUNT

Survey the area in which the game is to be played and list all of the scientific things it contains, whether of a general nature or for a game designed for a specialized topic area. Then prepare for each individual or "team" engaging in the game a list of ten or more suitable items, such as that shown in Figure 10-4, to be collected from the specified environment. Points may be assigned for each item on the list, with the team whose collection rates the highest score being named the winner.

ACTIVITY: PLAYING A GAME OF *WILDLIFE LOTTO*

Divide six cards, each about 12.5 cm. by 20 cm., into nine sections of equal size. Mark the center section WILDLIFE LOTTO and print the name of a different wildlife form in each of the remaining eight sections. Prepare all six cards such that no two are alike.

Cut twelve file cards, each about 7 cm. by 13 cm., into quarters and glue a wildlife stamp, each depicting a different

SCIENCE TREASURE HUNT

In the field environment you will be expected to collect:

Items	Point Value
6 different kinds of leaves from trees	6
2 different flowers	2
2 different fruits	2
2 crawling insects	2
2 flying insects	2
2 worms	2
4 different rock specimens	4
a soil sample made of 3 distinct layers	3
a small branch from a flowering shrub	1
a non-green plant specimen	1
TOTAL POSSIBLE SCORE	25

Figure 10-4. A Sample Treasure Hunt Card

form of wildlife, to the front of each small card. Then have anywhere from two to six players, each with a playing card in front of him, sit at a table with the picture cards stacked in a face-down position in the center of the table. Allow one player to select a card from the top of the stack and place it face-up on the table. Without any comments being made, the player who is first to recognize the picture as a wildlife form whose name is on his card may claim the picture card and place it over the space with the corresponding name. If a card is not claimed, it is returned to the bottom of the stack. Cards may be turned over, one at a time and by players in rotation, until all sections of one playing card have been covered with picture cards. The first player to cover his card completely and correctly with picture cards is the winner of the game of WILDLIFE LOTTO.

ACTIVITY: IDENTIFYING CONSTELLATIONS

Prepare thirty 13 cm. by 18 cm. cards, each with the outline of a different constellation drawn on the front and the correct identification of the constellation on the back of the card. One student will act as the leader. He will flash a card to each member of the group, individually. If the classmate identifies the constellation correctly he will remain in the game. If he makes an error he will be eliminated from the game. The student who stays in the game the longest will be adjudged the winner.

ACTIVITY: PLAYING A GAME OF
STEP ON MY SHADOW

On a sunny day while out-of-doors try to keep your classmates from stepping on your shadow. If your shadow is stepped on, then it will be your turn to be "It" and to try to step on someone else's shadow. The shadow-stepping is thus passed on from one player to another. Recalling how shadows are made, plan your strategy to avoid having your shadow stepped on and for succeeding in stepping on the shadow made by someone else.

ACTIVITY: PLAYING A GAME OF
METRIC BASEBALL

Draw a large baseball diamond on a large piece of poster board which can be attached to a bulletin board during the game of *Metric Baseball* being played between boys and girls in the class. Also provide each team with different colored markers on which can be placed numbers to identify individual team players. Pins or thumbtacks can be used to maintain the position of each player's marker on the diamond. Type a series of metric questions on 8 cm. by 13 cm. file cards in a sufficient number to allow for the following distribution:

one-question cards, designated as "singles"—50 percent

two-question cards, designated as "doubles"—30 percent

three-question cards, designated as "triples"—15 percent

four-question cards, designated as "home runs"—5 percent

After teams have been selected, determine the line-ups for players at bat. Then designate one person to act as a scorekeeper and another to be the umpire, who will resolve any problems that arise.

Rules of the Game:

1. Each team member, during his turn at bat, will be allowed to select a question card from a well-shuffled stack. As soon as an error is made the player at bat will be retired and the used card will be placed on the bottom of the stack.

2. A one-part question, if answered correctly, will advance the batter to first base. Any teammates already on base will also advance one base. If the answer given is incorrect, the player at bat will be retired and any players on base will maintain their positions.

3. A two-part question, if answered correctly, will advance the batter to second base. Any teammates already on a base will also advance two bases. If only the first part of the question is answered correctly, a player on base will advance one base but the batter will be retired. If the first part of the question is answered incorrectly, no moves are made and the batter is OUT.

4. If a player at bat selects a three-part question, he must answer all three parts correctly to run for a "triple," and bat in all other team members already on base. If only the first part of his question is answered correctly, a team member on base is advanced one base. If only the first and second parts of a question are answered correctly, a teammate already on base will advance two bases.

5. If a player selects a card with a four-part question, he must answer correctly all four parts to make a home run

and bat in all teammates on base as well. Answering the first part correctly will advance a teammate on base one base; answering the first and second parts of his question correctly will advance teammates on base two bases; and answering the first three parts of his question correctly will bring home any of his teammates already on base.

6. Each team will remain at bat until three batters have struck out.

7. The team with the highest score will be the winner.

For a game of METRIC BASEBALL, sample question cards for one-, two-, three-, and four-part questions follow.

SINGLE: The distance traveled by a school bus taking students to visit a Science Fair at a school in the next town would probably be measured in
                    X 1. kilometers
                         2. centimeters
                         3. millimeters
                         4. decimeters

DOUBLE: The standard unit of mass in the metric system is the
                         1. meter
                    X 2. kilogram
                         3. liter
                         4. cubic centimeter

The gram is about
                    X 1. 0.001 times as heavy as the kilogram
                         2. 1000 times as heavy as the kilogram
                         3.   100 times as heavy as the kilogram
                         4.   10 times as heavy as the kilogram

TRIPLE: The largest size bottle of Coke, 7-UP, or Pepsi purchased at a grocery store contains
                         1. 1   l.
                    X 2. 2   l.

    3. 0.5 l.
    4. 1.5 l.

If 200-ml. servings from this large size bottle are poured into paper cups, this will provide enough to serve how many students?

    1. Fifty
    2. Twenty
X 3. Ten
    4. Five

If the Coke is poured from this large size bottle to a half-gallon milk carton, the Coke would

X 1. Fill the milk carton with a little left over.
    2. Fill the milk carton exactly.
    3. Fill the milk carton halfway.
    4. Fill the milk carton almost to the top.

HOME RUN:The standard unit for measuring length in the metric system is the

    1. millimeter
    2. centimeter
X 3. meter
    4. kilometer

The smallest unit on most metric rulers is called a

X 1. millimeter
    2. meter
    3. centimeter
    4. decimeter

Ten millimeters make up the next largest metric unit called a

    1. meter
    2. decimeter
    3. dekameter
X 4. centimeter

The head of a thumbtack has a diameter of about

X 1. 1 cm.
   2. 1 mm.
   3. 1 m.
   4. 0.1 m.

ACTIVITIES INVOLVING A POTPOURRI OF SCIENTIFIC THINGS TO DO

A potpourri of science *fun* activities with take-home features have some very worthwhile long-range benefits. Those which can be recalled for the sheer enjoyment they provided will prompt students to share them with others; those whose patterns can be readily adapted to a new topic will afford opportunities for students to use ingenuity and resourcefulness in planning and conducting their leisure-time activity; and those which have been sources of much personal pleasure can easily become focal points for on-going science activities. In all, student curiosity and interest in science may be kept alive and well-nurtured as students engage in activities they enjoy. The result is the perpetuation of a positive outlook on science and the encouragement for students to look forward with anticipation to continuing the program of science activities in the next school year.

Facilities available to students for engaging in activities while away from school are naturally limited, and anything which is too involved would act to deter rather than to motivate and encourage participation in the activity. Activities with potential "carry-over into the summer vacation period" value are designed with a three-point focus:

1. They are suitable for students to perform with spontaneity.
2. They require the employment of only a minimum of the simplest of materials.

3. They appeal to students as sources of fun and enjoyment.

ACTIVITY: MAKING STICK FIGURES APPEAR TO MOVE

Cut a piece of white paper which measures 9 cm. wide and 28 cm. long and fold the paper across the center to make two sheets each 14 cm. long. Place the folded edge at the left and draw a stick figure in the center of the upper sheet. On the lower sheet draw the same figure in a slightly different stage of motion. Both figures should be facing up, with figure 1 directly above figure 2.

Starting at the open edge on the right, roll the upper fold of paper around a pencil, as shown in Figure 10-5, so that the curling of the upper sheet causes stick figure 2 to come into

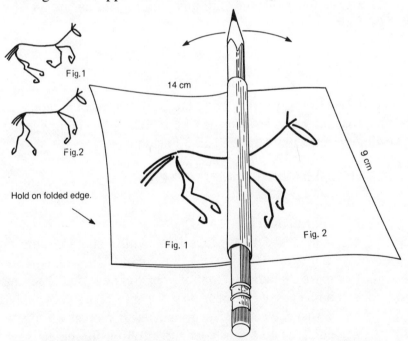

Figure 10-5. Making stick figures appear to move

view. Now move the pencil rapidly back and forth over the upper fold of paper and watch the figure appear to move.

ACTIVITY: ESTIMATING THE TEMPERATURE

On a warm summer evening listen to the sound of a chirping tree cricket. Using a stopwatch or other timing device count the number of chirps made in a 15-second period. Then add 39 to this number to calculate the temperature in degrees Fahrenheit.

For example:

If the number of chirps per 15 second is   29
Add   39
The estimated temperature is   68° F.

Then, to convert the Fahrenheit temperature reading to Celsius, subtract 32 and multiply the remaining number by 5/9. In this case, for 68° F.,

$$68 - 32 = 36$$
$$36 \times 5/9 = 20$$

Thus, 68° F. corresponds to 20° C.

The extreme sensitivity that tree crickets have to temperature changes provides a means by which an amazingly good estimate of the temperature can be made.

ACTIVITY: DEMONSTRATING PUZZLES
AND PUZZLERS

I. HOLE-IN-THE-HAND
Roll a sheet of paper into a tube about 3 cm. in diameter. Holding the tube with your right hand, place the tube in front of your right eye and, keeping both eyes open, focus on some object, such as a clock, across the room. Keep your left eye open while you continue to focus your attention on the object seen through the "telescope." Now move your left hand, with the palm open and facing you, so that the outside

edge of your hand rests along the side of the tube. Observe that you now appear to have a hole in the palm of your left hand and the object at a distance appears to be seen in that hole.

II. FLOATING FINGER

Keeping both eyes open, focus your attention on a distant object. While still focusing your attention on the far object touch together the tips of your two index fingers, about 15 cm. in front of your face. Slowly draw your fingers slightly apart and observe the extra piece of finger that appears to be floating in midair. By wiggling your fingers slightly you can cause the little piece of finger to perform some interesting acrobatics. To make the floating finger disappear, change your focus and focus in on the fingers in front of your face instead of the far wall.

III. PERPETUAL STAIRCASE

On a piece of plain white paper carefully reproduce the diagram shown in Figure 10-6. Examine the diagram. Then, starting at the left side of the diagram, follow the steps upward, tracing a pathway completely around the figure. Repeat the tour around the

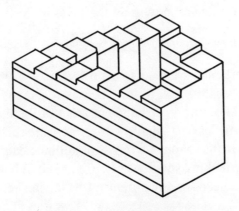

Figure 10-6.   An optical illusion

figure several times. Now reverse your direction: starting again at the left, follow the steps in the opposite direction, in a downward journey. Try to figure out why it is that if you travel in one direction you will always be going up yet never reach the top, and if you travel in the opposite direction you will always be going down, yet never reach the bottom. The figure leads you in an unending journey either in an upward or in a downward direction.

ACTIVITY: WRITING AND DECODING AN INVISIBLE MESSAGE

In half a test tube of water dissolve some sodium thiocyanate until no more will go into solution. Using this colorless liquid and a clean pen write a secret message on a white card. Since the message was written with a colorless solution, the card will appear to be blank.

When ready to "decode" the invisible message, prepare a solution of ferric chloride in half a test tube of water. Then reveal the secret message by saturating a cotton ball with ferric chloride solution and wiping it gently across the written message on the surface of the card. A chemical reaction occurring between the two chemicals produces a red-pigmented iron compound so you can now read the message in *red*.

ACTIVITY: PRODUCING A SHADOW SHOW

In a darkened room, use a projector or a bright lamp to illuminate a white background such as a screen, a wall, or a sheet. Then, holding your hands in front of the light source so that they will cast a shadow on the screen, make some "shadows" in the shape of animals or animal heads for others to identify. Try making shadows of birds, a rabbit head, a chicken head, a dog's head, or any other figure that can be shown on the screen.

ACTIVITY: DECORATING EMPTY EGGSHELLS

Obtain some jumbo-sized white eggs to be decorated. First place the eggs in a bowl of hot water to warm them slightly. Then remove the eggs one at a time and evacuate the shells: dry off an egg with soft tissue; use a darning needle or tapestry needle to puncture a 0.25-cm. hole through the shell at the egg's narrow end and a 0.5-cm. hole through the shell at its wider end; rotate the needle inside the shell to pierce the yolk; and, holding the egg above a bowl on a table, press your lips to the smaller hole and blow gently until all of the material within the shell has been blown through the large hole and collected in the bowl.

Carefully wash the empty shells with warm water and dry the outside surface with soft tissue, setting the delicate shells in an empty egg carton for catching any remaining drips. When the shells are clean and dry they are ready to decorate. Place an empty shell on a padded surface and mark it with a design previously worked out on paper or mapped out on the eggshell surface. Then color the design, using colored pens, pencils, ink, paint, sequins, and decorative tape as needed. Finally, attach small pieces of thread or ribbon for suspending the decorated eggshells or arrange them in an attractive display on velvet, in a box, or in a basket.

ACTIVITY: HOLDING A PARACHUTE MEET

Carefully slit down one side of a plastic garment bag of the type used by dry cleaners. Lay the resulting plastic sheet flat on the floor or table and measure off a regular six-sided figure. With scissors, cut out this hexagon and use it for a parachute canopy. Tape a piece of nylon sewing thread to each corner of the canopy and allow suspension lines about three-fourths as long as the diameter of the canopy. Then hold the corners of the canopy together and pull the free ends of the suspension threads together. After making sure that all lines are the same length, tie

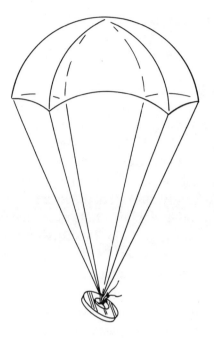

Figure 10-7.   Six-sided toy parachute

their free ends together and attach a washer or a nut to the knot. (See Figure 10-7.)

From an elevated position, preferably in calm air, drop the parachute and time its descent. For a competitive activity have classmates make individual parachutes, using different designs, different materials, different canopy shapes, and different materials and lengths for suspension lines. In a parachute meet, value points can be given for parachute performance.

ACTIVITY: HOLDING A KITE-FLYING CONTEST

On a windy day hold a kite-flying contest for students to display their skills using kites of their own construction. A basic two-stick flat kite as shown in Figure 10-8 can be made easily, using simple materials. Cut two lightweight sticks, one 76 cm., the other 88 cm. in length. Cut notches at both ends of both

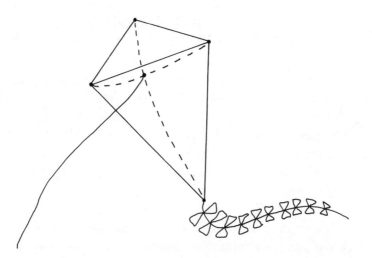

Figure 10-8.   A basic 2-stick flat kite

sticks. To indicate where the sticks should cross, mark the longer stick at a point 22 cm. from one end. Similarly mark the shorter stick at its midpoint. Then cross the sticks, where marked, and glue them together.

Run a framing string around the frame, connecting the outer ends of the sticks and using the notches to make the frame tight and secure. Lay the frame on a large piece of paper and cut the paper in the shape of the frame, allowing an overlap of 2 cm. on each side. Fold this overlap of the paper over the framing string and paste the paper into position.

After the paste has dried, tie a string from one end to the other of the cross stick, allowing 15 cm. of slack in the string. Similarly attach a string from end to end of the longer stick, again allowing for 15 cm. of slack. Where these two strings cross, tie one end of a kite string that is also attached to a reel. Make a kite tail by tying some brightly colored ribbons or bows to a long string. Then attach the tail to the bottom of the kite and fly the kite on a windy day.

ACTIVITIES INVOLVING
LEISURE TIME AND REFERENCE READING

Books can open doors to an understanding of science. They nurture student curiosity; they are both a starting point and a follow-up for many hands-on activities; they support the active three-dimensional experiences that are the crux of student inquiry and investigative activities; and they provide a source of pleasure and enjoyment while expanding a student's fund of scientific information and contributing to the development of his attitudes toward science in a positive way.

The reading activities for elementary school students are, of course, directly related to their interests. Curiosity about a captured insect encourages reference reading to learn of its identity and life habits, excitement concerning a student-performed experiment or demonstration suggests research into specific topic areas which give breadth and depth to the study, and exploratory reading stimulates new interests while expanding the perspective of existing ones.

The use of a variety of science books can be enhanced by encouraging extensive reading in both the central library and the classroom resource center, and in students' growing personal libraries. Reading activities promoted throughout the school year reach a peak in June when students have developed a certain independence and responsibility for self-learning. The reading activity, once established, suggests an on-going summer activity program of voluntary reading for pleasure and enjoyment, and for great personal satisfaction.

A sampling of science books recommended for elementary school students is included in the list that follows.

BOOKS FOR CHILDREN

Abbott, Tucker, *Seashells of the World*. Racine, Wisc.: Western Publishing Co., 1962.

Anderson, Valerie, *Thinking Games 1*. Belmont, CA.: Pitman Learning Inc., 1980.

_____, *Thinking Games 2*. Belmont, CA.: Pitman Learning Inc., 1980.

Ardley, Neil, *Know Your Underwater Exploration*. Chicago, Ill.: Rand McNally & Co., 1977.

Bernath, Stefen, *Common Weeds Coloring Book*. New York: Dover Publishing Co., Inc., 1976.

_____, *Garden Flowers Coloring Book*. New York: Dover Publishing Co., Inc., 1975.

_____, *Herbs Coloring Book*. New York: Dover Publishing Co., Inc., 1977.

_____, *House Plants Coloring Book*. New York: Dover Publishing Co., Inc., 1976.

_____, *Tropical Fish Coloring Book*. New York: Dover Publishing Co., Inc., 1978.

Brown, Anne Ensign, *Wonders of Sea Horses*. New York: Dodd Mead & Co., 1979.

Carr, Marion, *Oceanography*. Golden Science Guide. Racine, Wisc.: Western Publishing Co., 1973.

Casanova, Richard and C. A. Healdsburg, *Illustrated Guide to Fossil Collecting*. Naturegraph Publishers, 1970.

D'Attillio, Anthony, *Seashore Life Coloring Book*. New York: Dover Publishing Co., Inc., 1973.

Fichter, George S., *Animals*. Golden Nature Guide. Racine, Wisc.: Western Publishing Co., 1973.

_____, *The Human Body*. Golden Exploring Earth Book. Racine, Wisc.: Western Publishing Co., 1977.

_____, *Insects*. Golden Exploring Earth Book. Racine, Wisc.: Western Publishing Co., 1975.

Fraser, Brunner A., *How to Have a Successful Aquarium*. Neptune N.J.: TFH Publications, Inc., 1974.

Hoffmeister, Donald F., *Zoo Animals*. Golden Guide Series. Racine, Wisc.: Western Publishing Co., 1967.

Hussong, Clara, *Birds*. Golden Exploring Earth Book. Racine, Wisc.: Western Publishing Co., 1973.

_____, *Nature Hikes*. Golden Exploring Earth Book. Racine, Wisc.: Western Publishing Co., Inc., 1973.

Kennedy, Paul E., *American Wild Flowers Coloring Book,* New York: Dover Publishing Co., Inc., 1971.

_____, *Audubon's Birds of America Coloring Book*. New York: Dover Publishing Co., Inc., 1974.

Lambert, David, *The World of Animals*. New York: Franklin Watts, Warwick Press, 1978.

Lauber, Patricia, *What's Hatching Out of That Egg?* New York: Crown Publishers Inc., 1979.

Livesey, Antony and Stephanie Thompson, *Know Your Wild Animals*. Chicago, Ill.: Rand McNally & Co., 1977.

Lyon, Jene, *Astronomy*. Golden Exploring Earth Book. Racine, Wisc.: Western Publishing Co., 1974.

Martin, Alice F. and Bertha M. Parker, *Dinosaurs*. Golden Exploring Earth Book. Racine, Wisc.: Western Publishing Co., 1973.

_____, *Rocks and Minerals*. Golden Exploring Earth Book. Racine, Wisc.: Western Publishing Co., 1974.

Meadows, David, *Know Your Dinosaurs*. Chicago, Ill.: Rand Mc Nally & Co., 1977.

Paton, John (ed.), *Children's Encyclopedia of Science*. Chicago, Ill.: Rand McNally & Co., 1977.

Rhodes, Frank, Herbert Zim, and Paul Schaffner, *Fossils*. Racine, Wisc.: Western Publishing Co., 1962.

Robert, Mervin F., *Your Terrarium*. Neptune, N.J.: TFH Publications, Inc., 1963.

Rogovin, Anne, *Let Me Do It!* New York: Lippincott and Crowell/Harper and Row, 1980.

Saunders, Graham D., *Spotter's Guide to Shells.* New York: Mayflower Books, 1979.

Sawyer, Roger W. and Robert A. Farmer, *New Ideas for Science Fair Projects.* New York: Arco Publishing Co., 1967.

Schlein, Miriam, *Lucky Porcupine.* Four Winds Press, 1980.

Schneider, Herman and Nina Schneider, *Science Fun For You In A Minute Or Two: Quick Science Experiments You Can Do.* New York: McGraw Hill Book Co., 1975.

Striker, Susan, *The Anti-Coloring Book of Exploring Space on Earth.* New York: Holt, Rinehart, and Winston, 1980.

Thompson, Stephanie, *Know Your Human Body.* Chicago, Ill.: Rand McNally & Co., 1977.

Victor, Joan Berg, *Tarantulas.* New York: Dodd Mead & Co., 1977.

Warner, Matt, *Flowers, Trees, and Gardening.* Golden Exploring Earth Book. Racine, Wisc.: Western Publishing Co., 1975.

———, *Reptiles and Amphibians.* Golden Exploring Earth Book. Racine, Wisc.: Western Publishing Co., 1974.

Wyler, Rose, *Science.* Golden Exploring Earth Book. Racine, Wisc.: Western Publishing Co., 1973.

Science activities can be not only fascinating and informative for elementary school students, but they can be sources of great *fun* and *enjoyment* as well. Those with take-home features have the added advantage of encouraging even greater student exposure to the world of science by projecting specific classroom activities into their lives away from school. Fun-type activities provide great motivation for learning in the most pleasurable way, and, in the teacher's repertoire of science activities, they are surely the most popular among elementary students.

BOOKS FOR TEACHERS

Abruscato, Joe and Jack Hassard, *The Whole Cosmos Catalog of Science Activities*. Santa Monica, CA: Goodyear Publishing Co., Inc., 1977.

Axelrod, Herbert R. and Leonard P. Schultz, *Handbook of Tropical Aquarium Fishes*. Neptune, N.J.: TFH Publications, Inc., 1978.

Benry, Ronald (ed.), *Ideas for Science Fair Projects*. New York: Arco Publishing Co., 1962.

Best, Richard L., *Living Arthropods in the Classroom*. Burlington, N.C.: Carolina Biological Supply Co., 1978.

Blackwelder, Sheila Kyser, *Science For All Seasons: Science Experiences For Young Children*. Englewood Cliffs, N.J.: Prentice-Hall, Inc., 1980.

Blaustein, Elliott H., *Anti-Pollution Projects*. New York: Arco Publishing Co., 1977. (Rev.)

Edmund Scientific Co., *Simplified Science Activities*. Barrington, N.J.: Edmund Scientific Co., Booklet No. 9896.

Hawley, Robert C. and Isabel L. Hawley, *Building Motivation In The Classroom*. Amherst, Mass.: Education Research Associates, 1979.

Jacobsen, Willard J. and Abby Barry Bergman, *Science for Children: A Book for Teachers*. Englewood Cliffs, N.J.: Prentice-Hall Inc., 1980.

Kaplan, Sandra N. et al, *Change for Children: Ideas and Activities for Individualized Learning*, Revised. Santa Monica, CA.: Goodyear Publishing Co., Inc., 1980.

Linn, Marcia C., "Free-Choice Experiences: How Do They Help Students Learn?" *Science Education* 64: 237-48; No. 2, 1980.

Maggs, Margaret Martin, *The Classroom Survival Book: A Practical Manual for Teachers*. New York: Franklin Watts, Warwick Press, 1980.

Newman, Thelma R., *Changeover - Breakthrough to Individualization*. Wayne, N.J.: Wayne Township Public Schools, Palisade Printing Co., 1976.

Pavlich, Vita and Eleanor Rosenast, *Do Something Different: Innovative Study Projects for Grades 4-7*. Belmont, CA.: Pitman Learning Inc., 1980.

Prentice-Hall, *The Curious Naturalist*. Englewood Cliffs, N.J.: Prentice-Hall, Inc., 1980.

Sawyer, Roger W. and Robert A. Farmer, *New Ideas for Science Fair Projects*. New York: Arco Publishing Co., 1967.

Wlodkowski, Raymond J., *Motivation and Teaching: A Practical Guide*. An N.E.A. Publication. West Haven, Conn.: N.E.A. Distribution Center, 1980.

Index